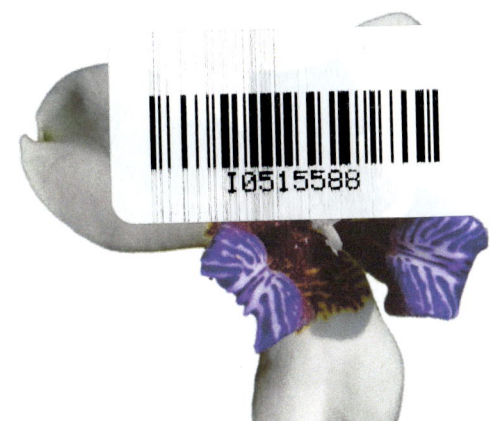

# Flowers Coloridas

book & photography by
Jodi Marie Fisher

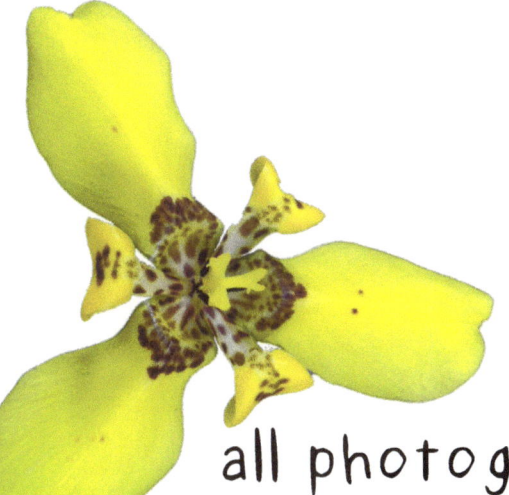

all photographs taken in Costa Rica

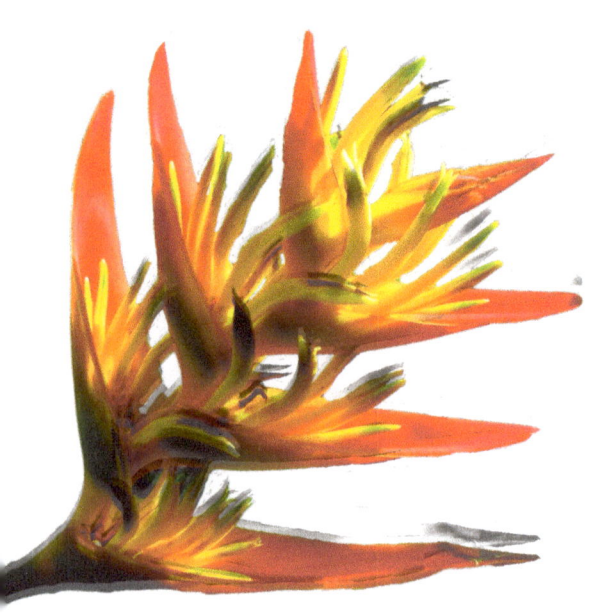

Copyright © 2018 Jodi Marie Fisher
Photography by Jodi Marie Fisher

All rights reserved. This book or any portion thereof may not be reproduced or used in any manner whatsoever without the express written permission of the publisher.

Printed in the United States of America
First Edition 2018
Flowers Coloridas
A Bilingual Book of Costa Rican Flower Photography

ISBN-13: 978-1979537498
ISBN-10: 1979537496

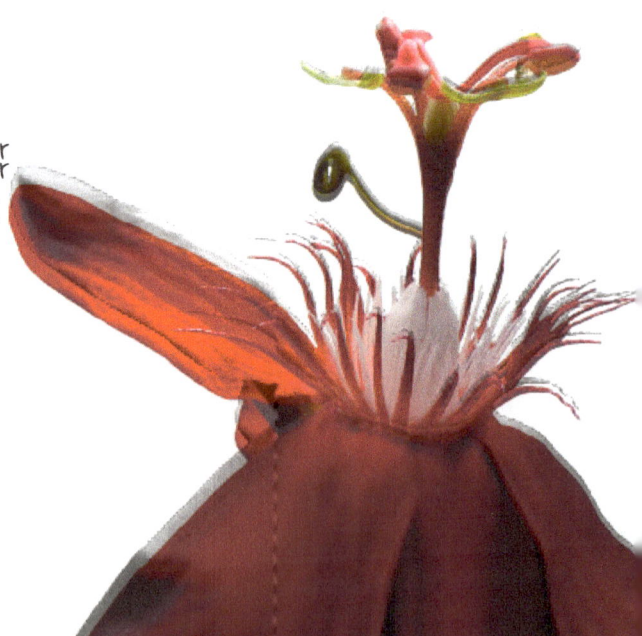

# Spanish Pronunciation Guide

Unlike English, the five vowels (A, E, I, O, U) only make five vowel sounds. Each vowel is always pronounced the same without any exceptions

- **A** — The letter A is always AH (like in the word awesome)
- **E** — The letter E is always A (like in the word baby)
- **I** — The letter I is always E (like in the word dream)
- **O** — The letter O is always OH (like in the word go)
- **U** — The letter U is always OOO (like in the word moon)

Many of the consonants in Spanish make the same sounds as the English letters, but the following letters are different in these ways

- **J** — The letter J makes an H sound (like in the word hug)
- **LL** — The double letter LL makes a Y sound in Spanish, but is actually pronounced like a J in Costa Rica
- **H** — The letter H is silent and doesn't make any sound at all
- **Ñ** — The letter Ñ that is an n with a swirly line above it is NY
- **C** — The letter C is K (like in the word cat) before the vowels A, O, and U and S (like in the word city) before the vowels E and I
- **G** — The letter G is G (like in the word girl) before the vowels A, O, and U and H (like in the word help) before the vowels E and I
- **GU** — The combination of the letters GU is pronounced G (like in the word good) and you don't pronounce the U
- **QU** — The combination of the letters QU is pronounced K (like in the word kiss) and you don't pronounce the U
- **Y** — The letter Y is simply pronounced as E when it's by itself, but as a consonant it is pronounced like the Y in English
- **R** — The R in spanish is flipped and the double R (RR) is rolled

This is a
red flower.

Esta es
una flor roja.

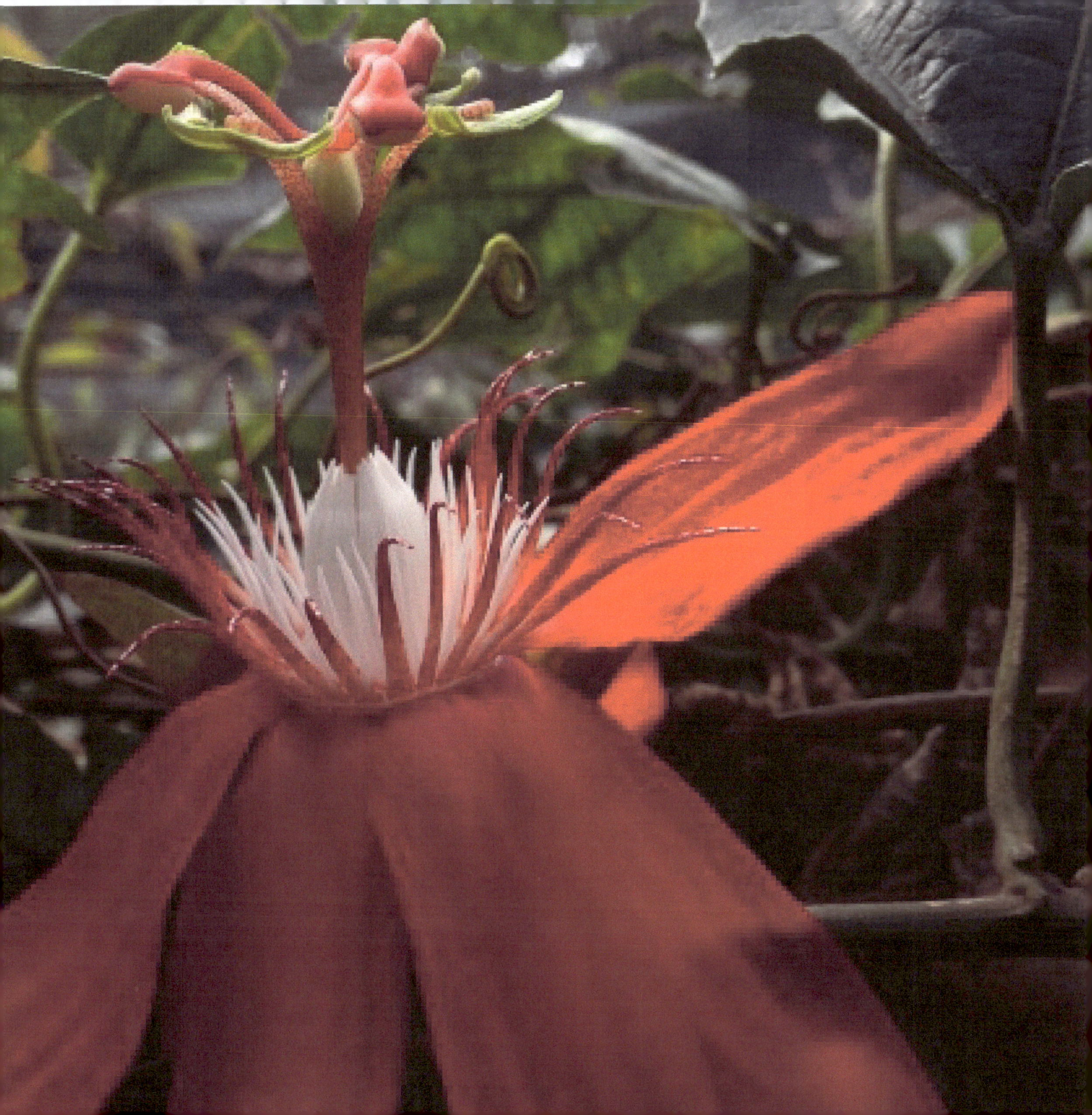

This is another red flower.

Esta es otra flor roja.

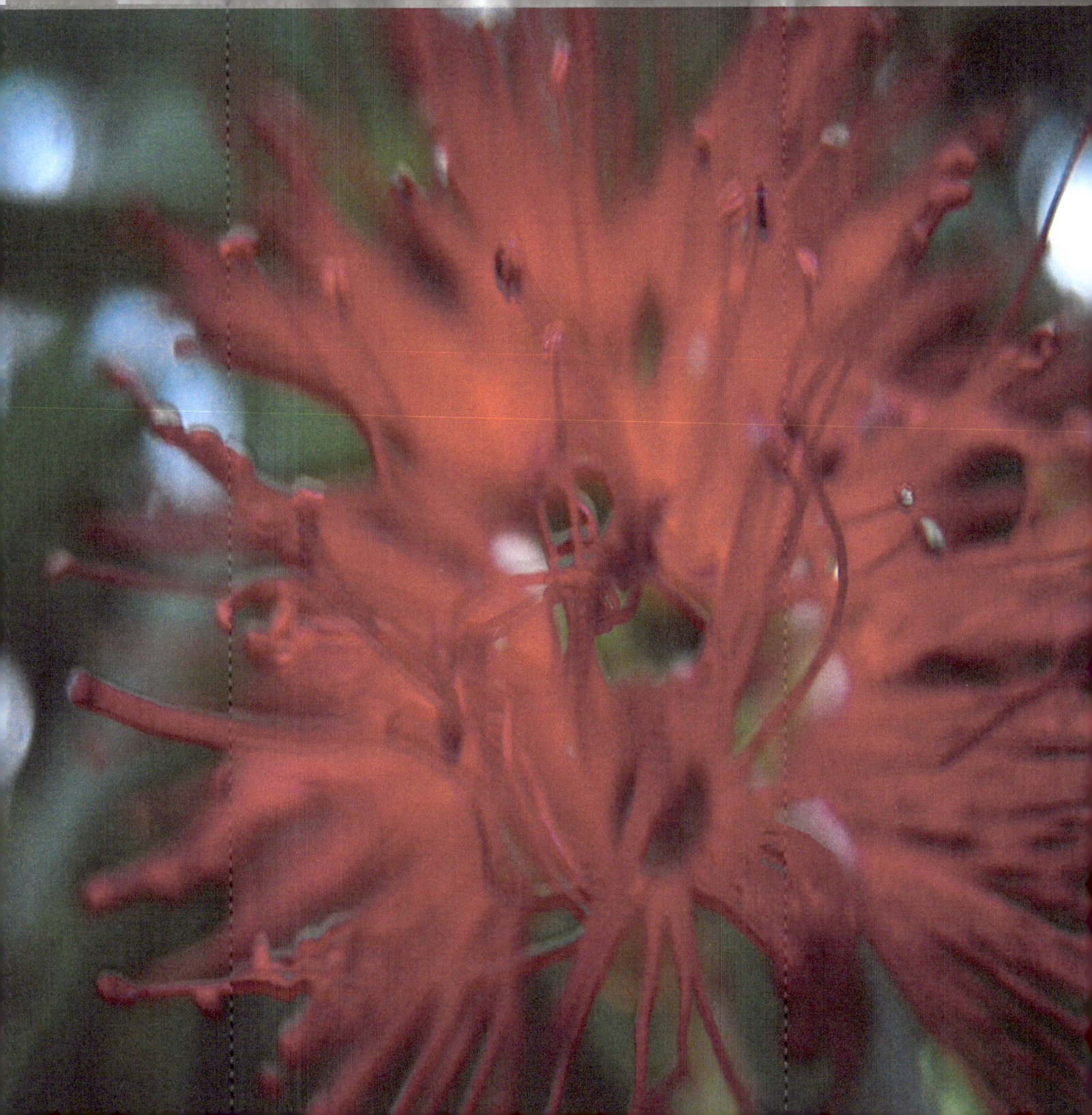

This is a bright red flower.

Esta es una flor de color rojo brillante.

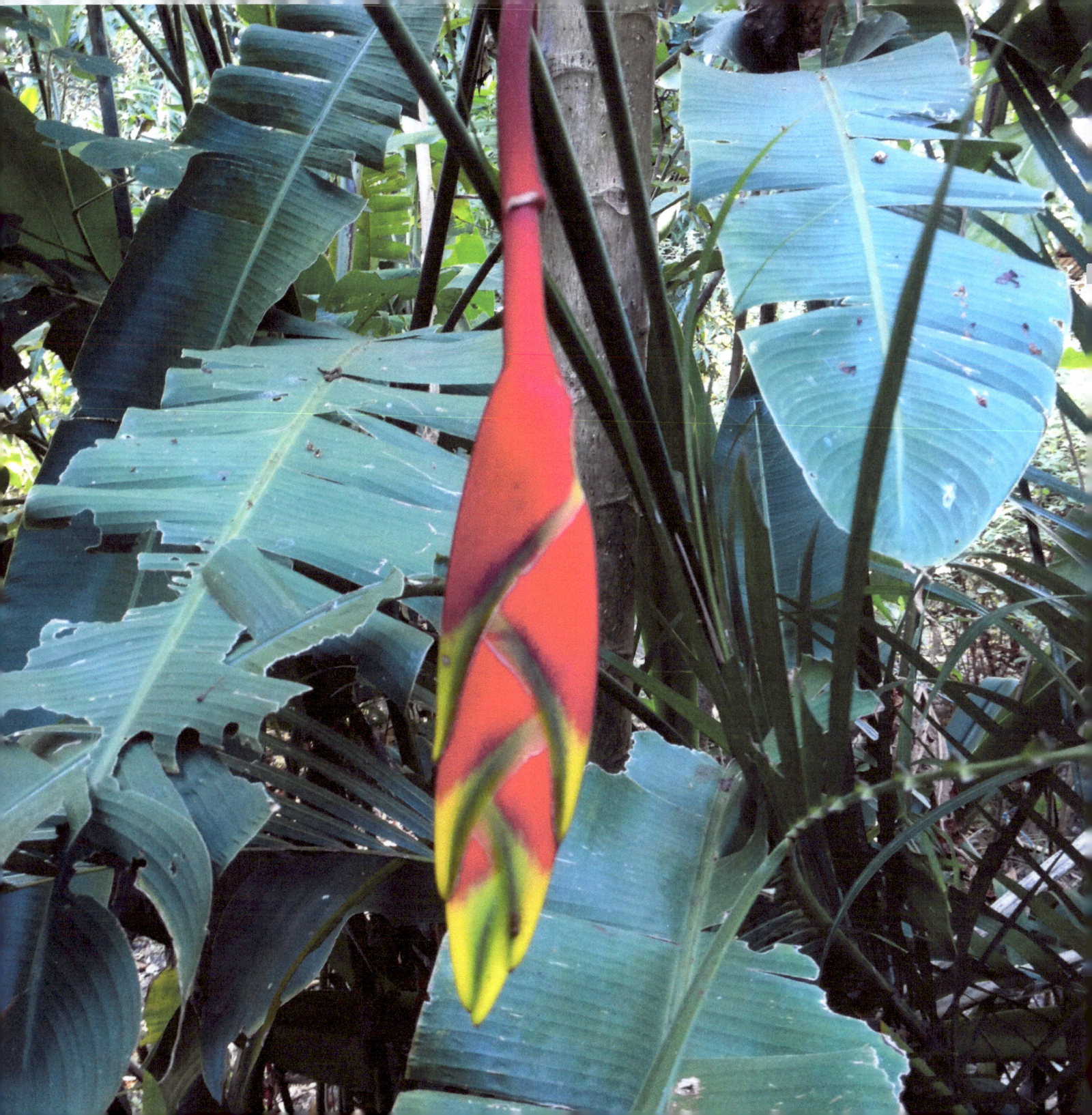

These are orange flowers.

Estas son flores anaranjadas.

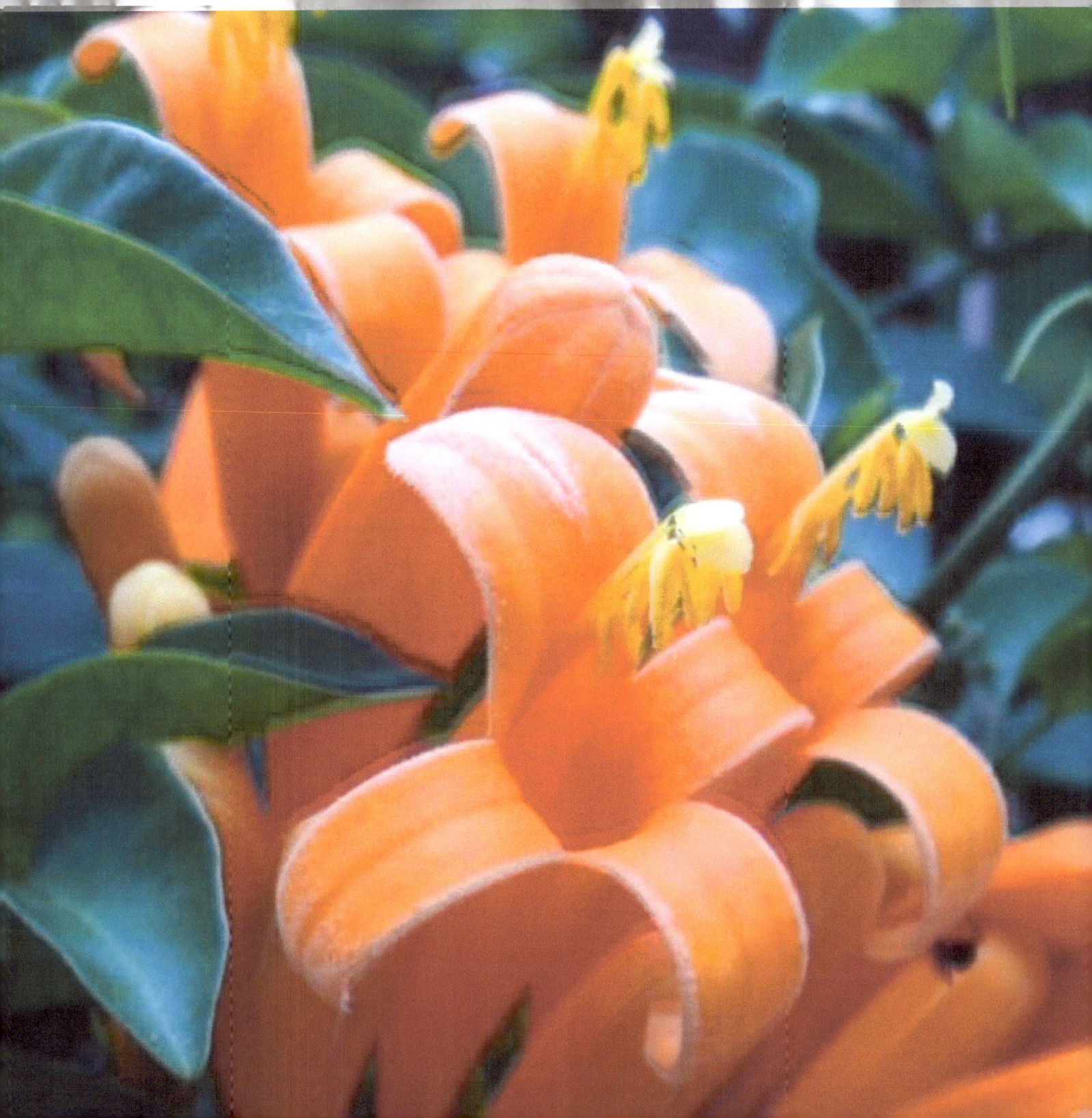

This is an orange flower.

Esta es una flor anaranjada.

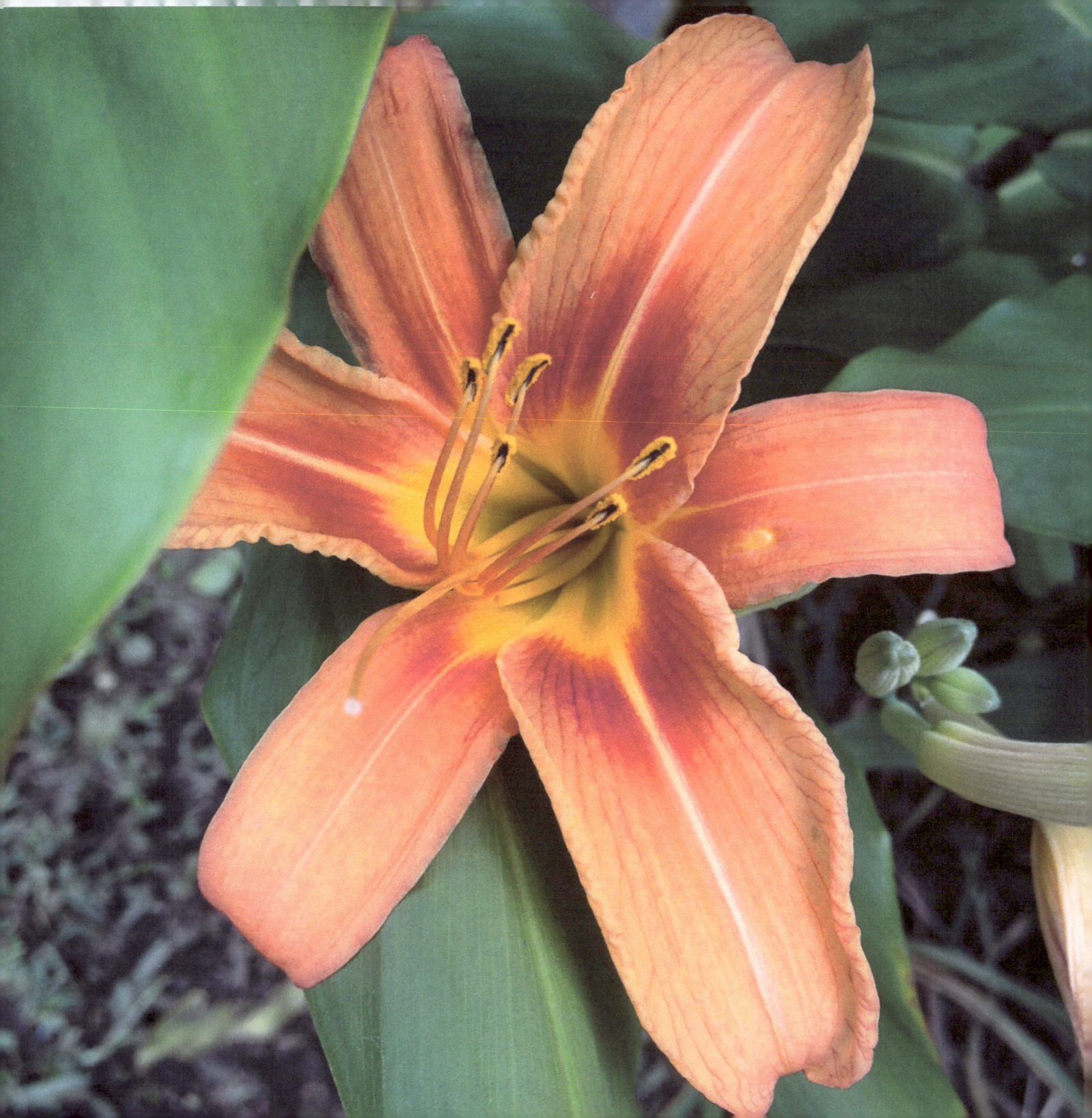

These are more orange flowers.

Estas son mas flores anaranjadas.

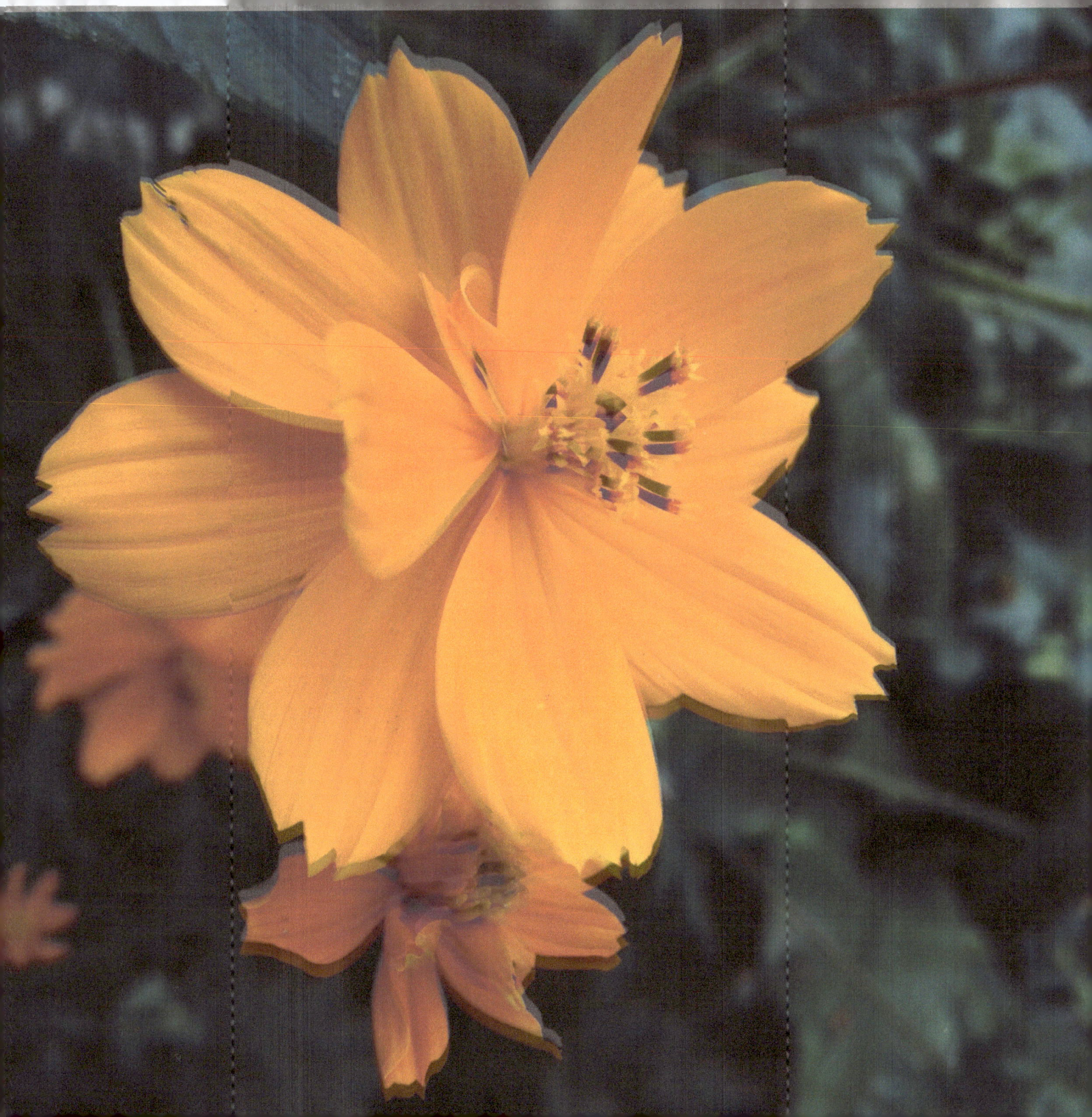

This is a yellow flower.

Esta es una flor amarilla.

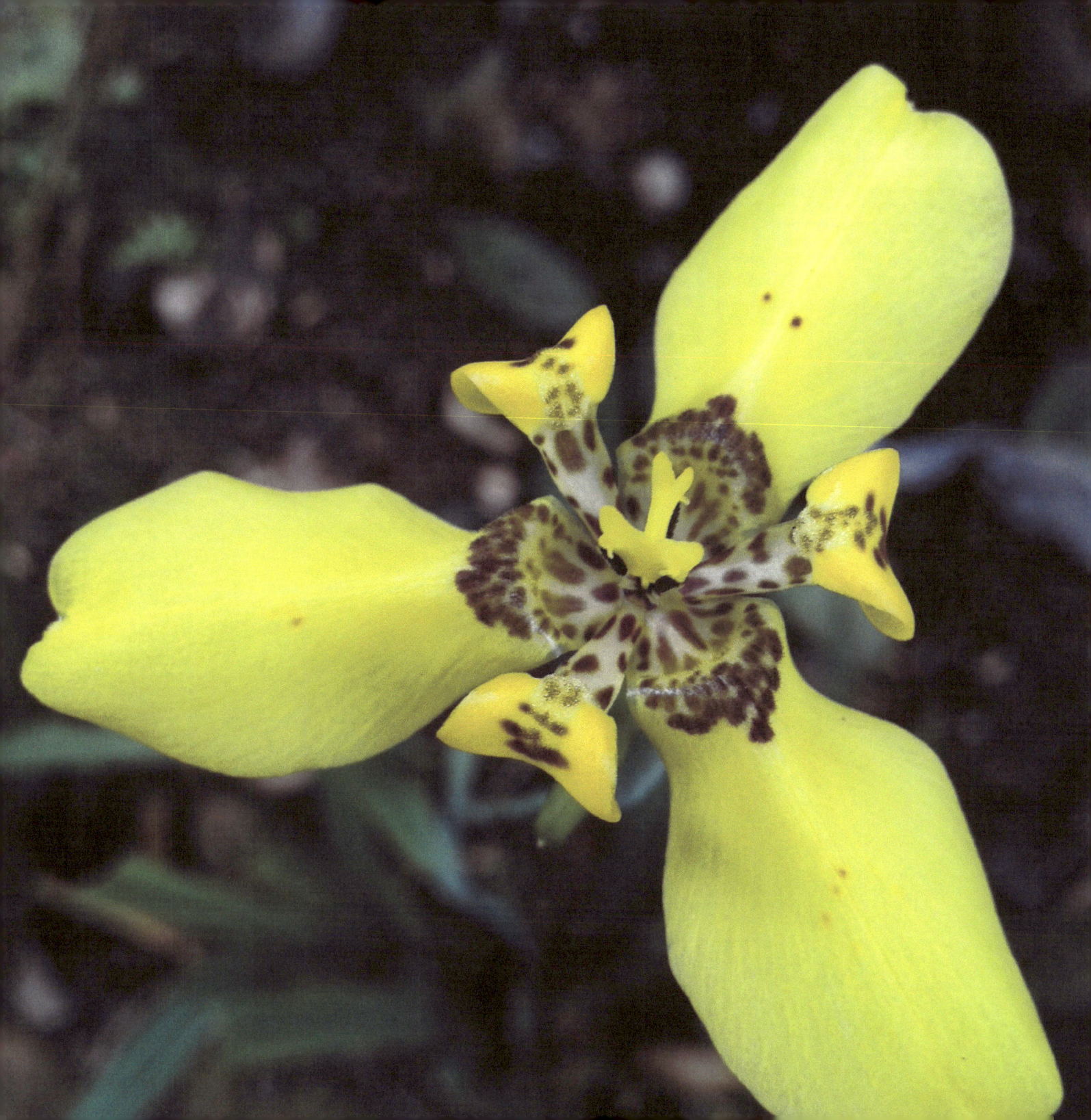

This is a bright yellow flower.

Esta es una flor de color amarillo brillante.

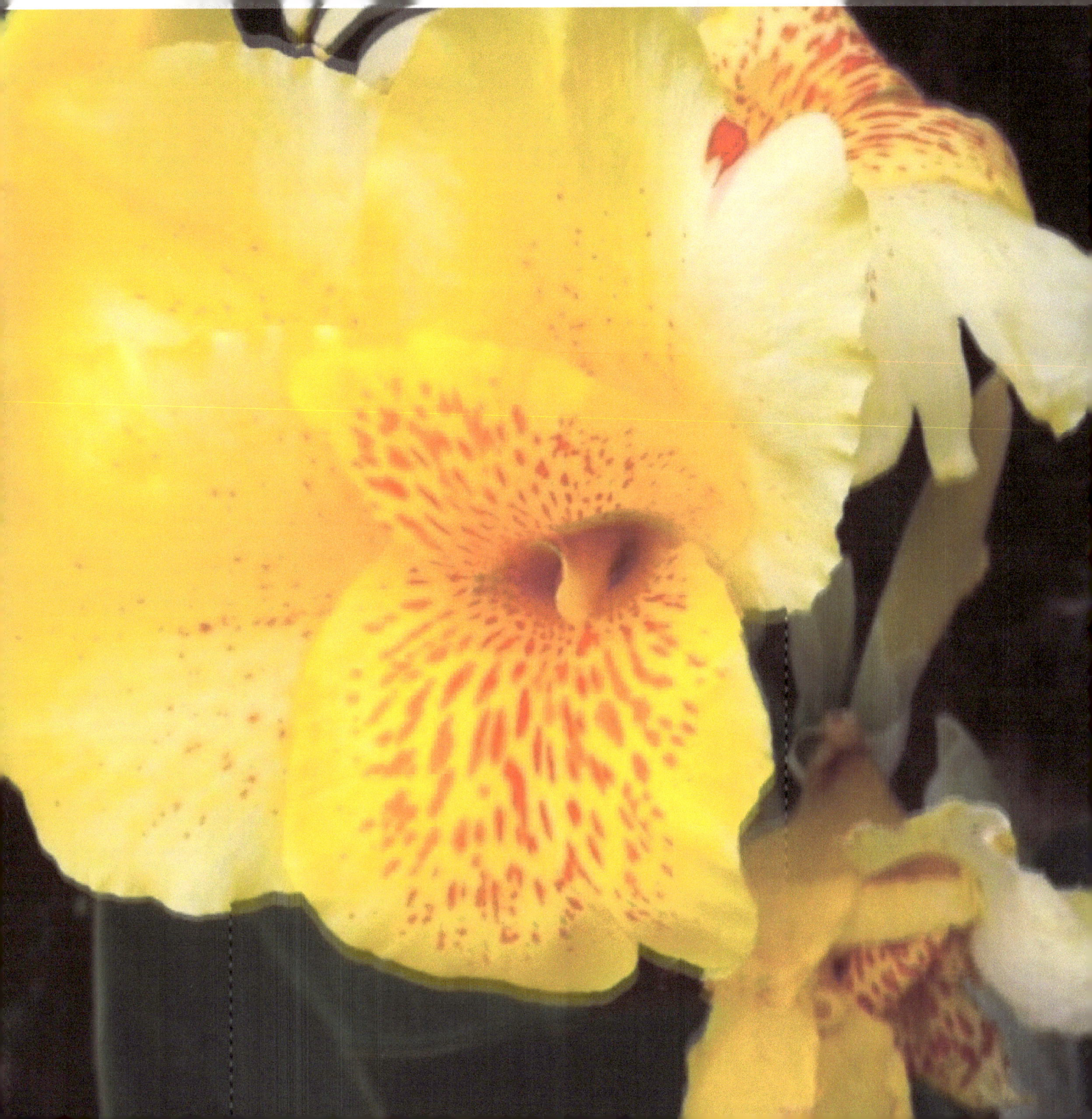

This is another yellow flower.

Esta es otra flor amarilla.

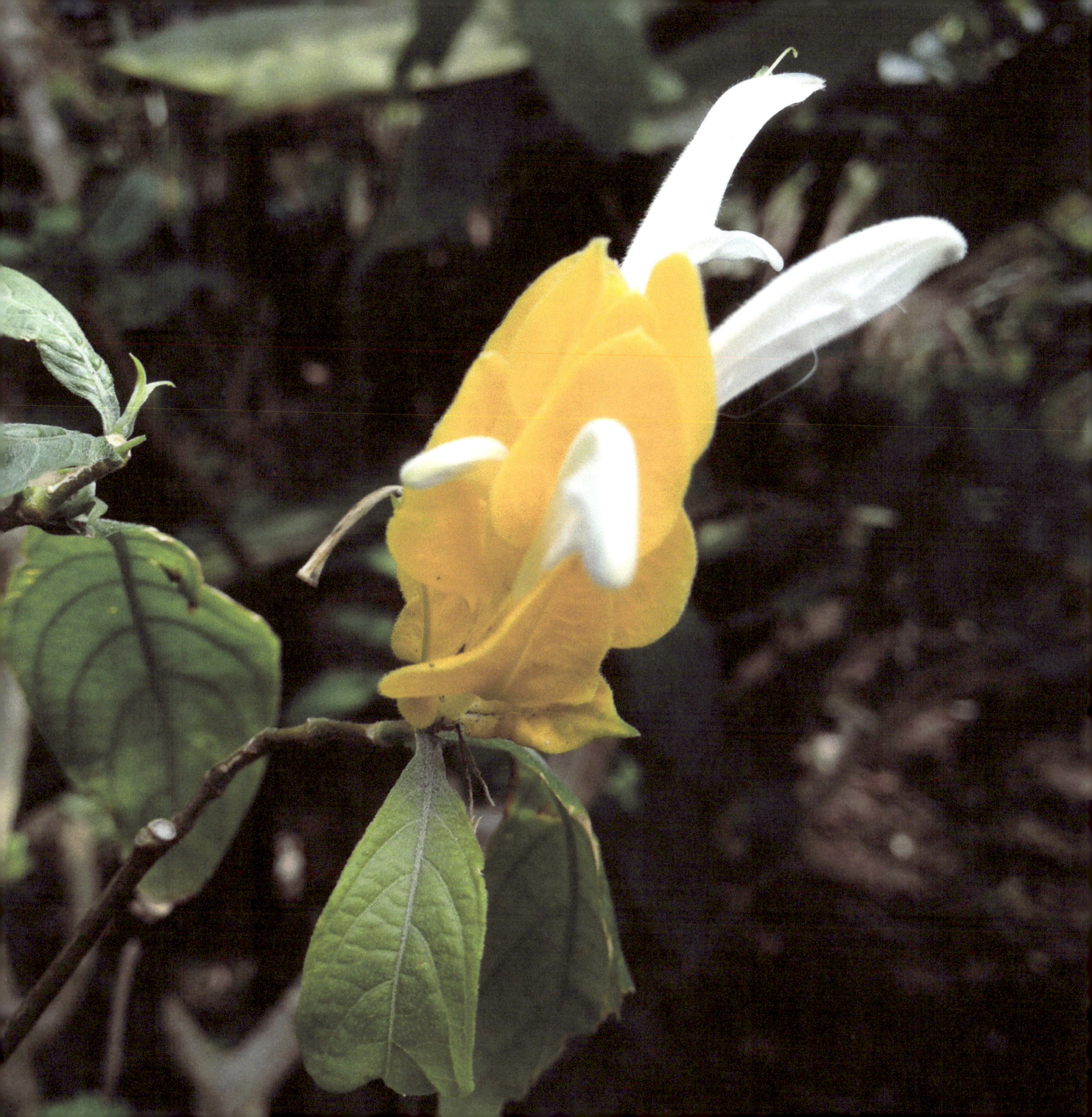

This is a light green flower.

Esta es una flor de color verde claro.

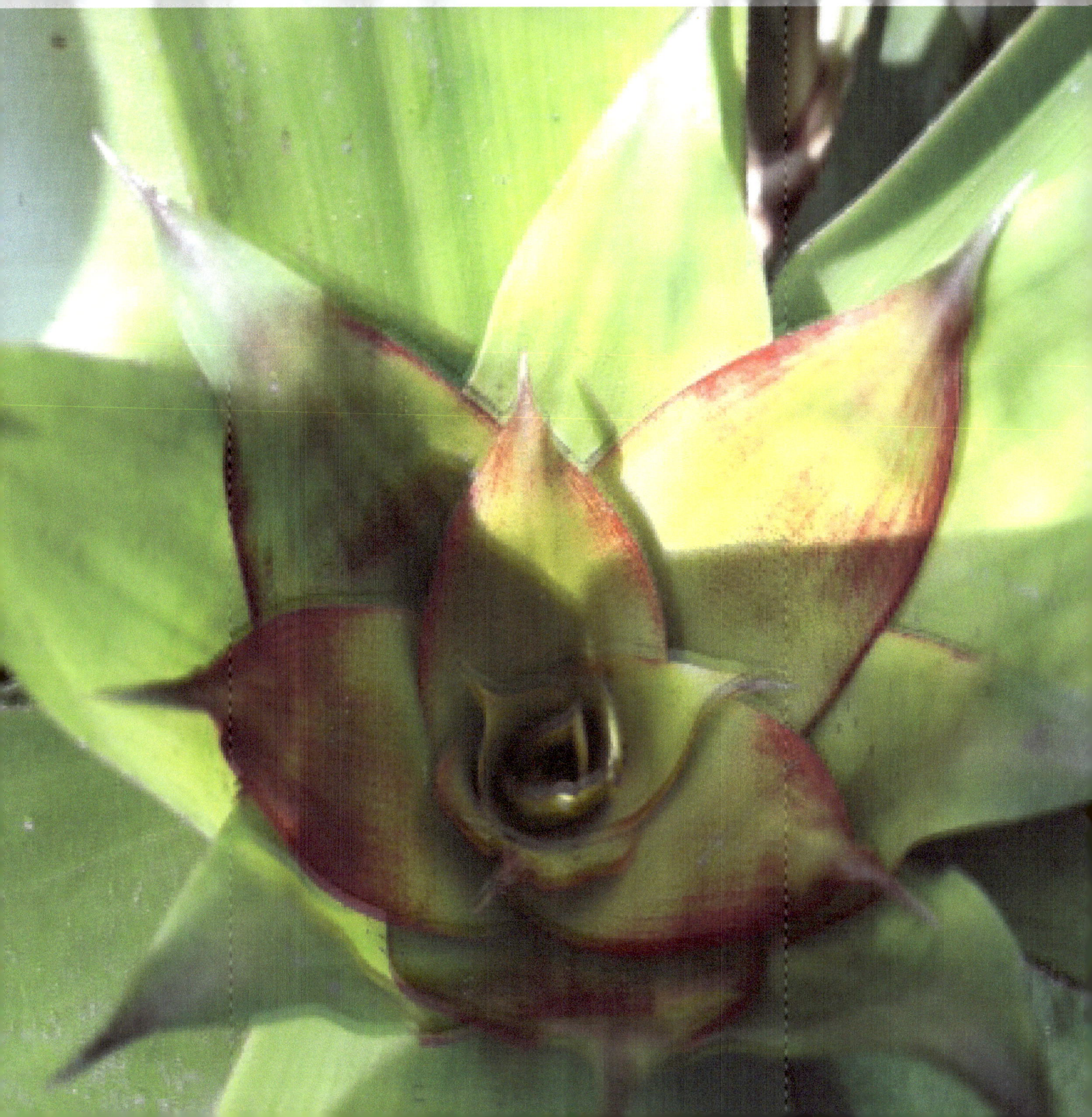

This is a striped green flower.

Esta es una flor verde de rayas.

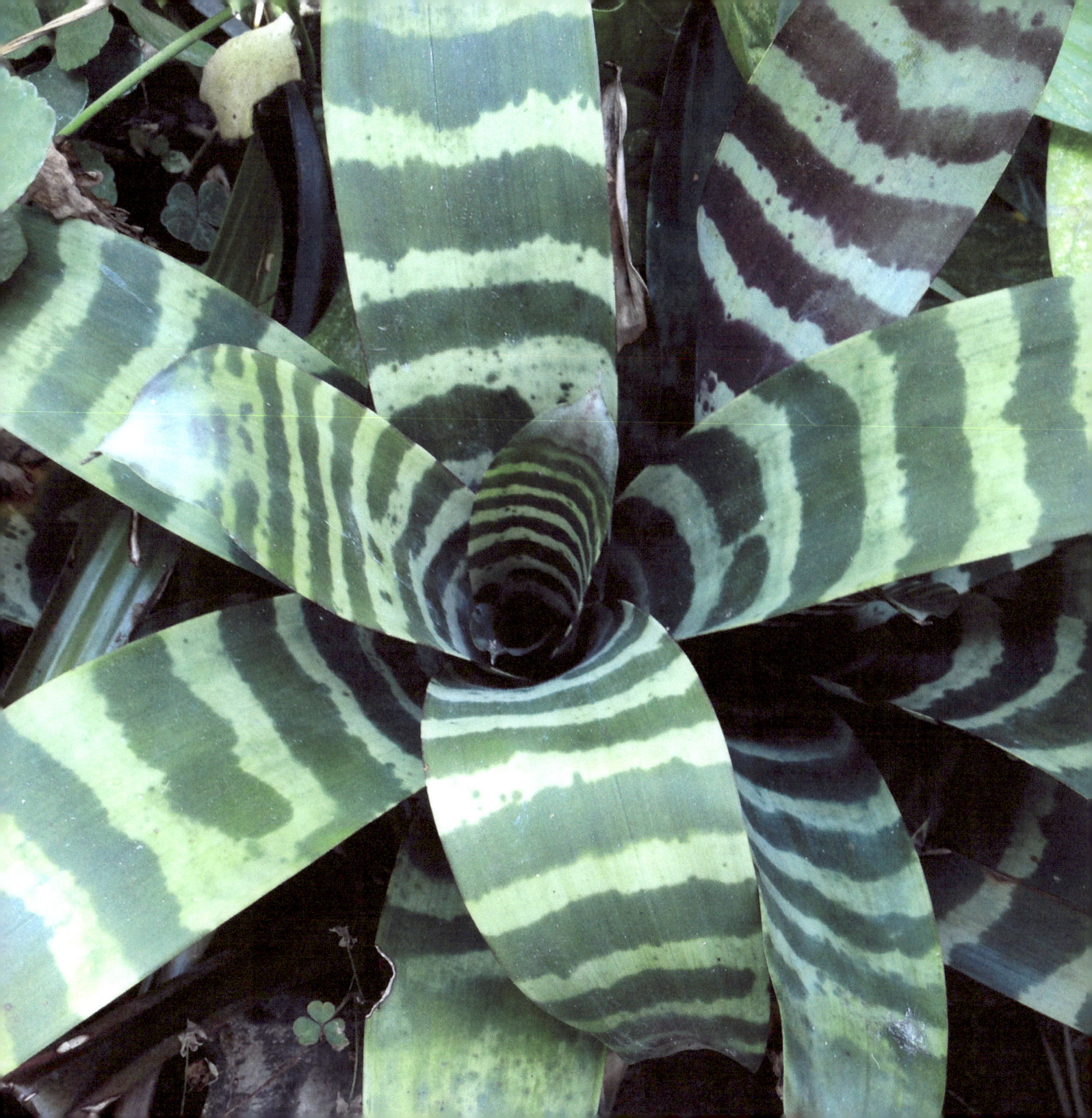

These are green flowers.

Estas son flores verdes.

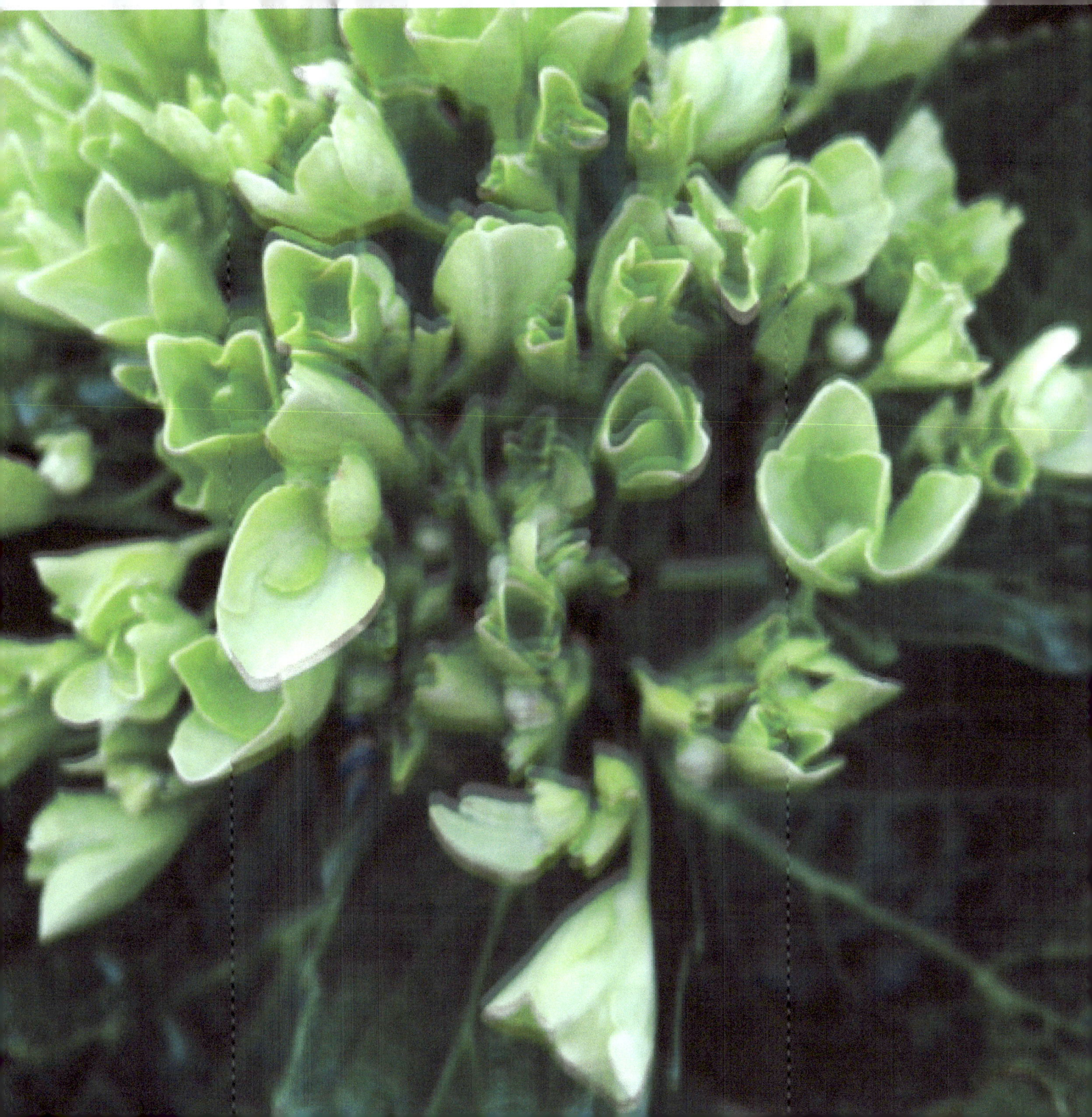

This is a blue flower.

Esta es una flor azul.

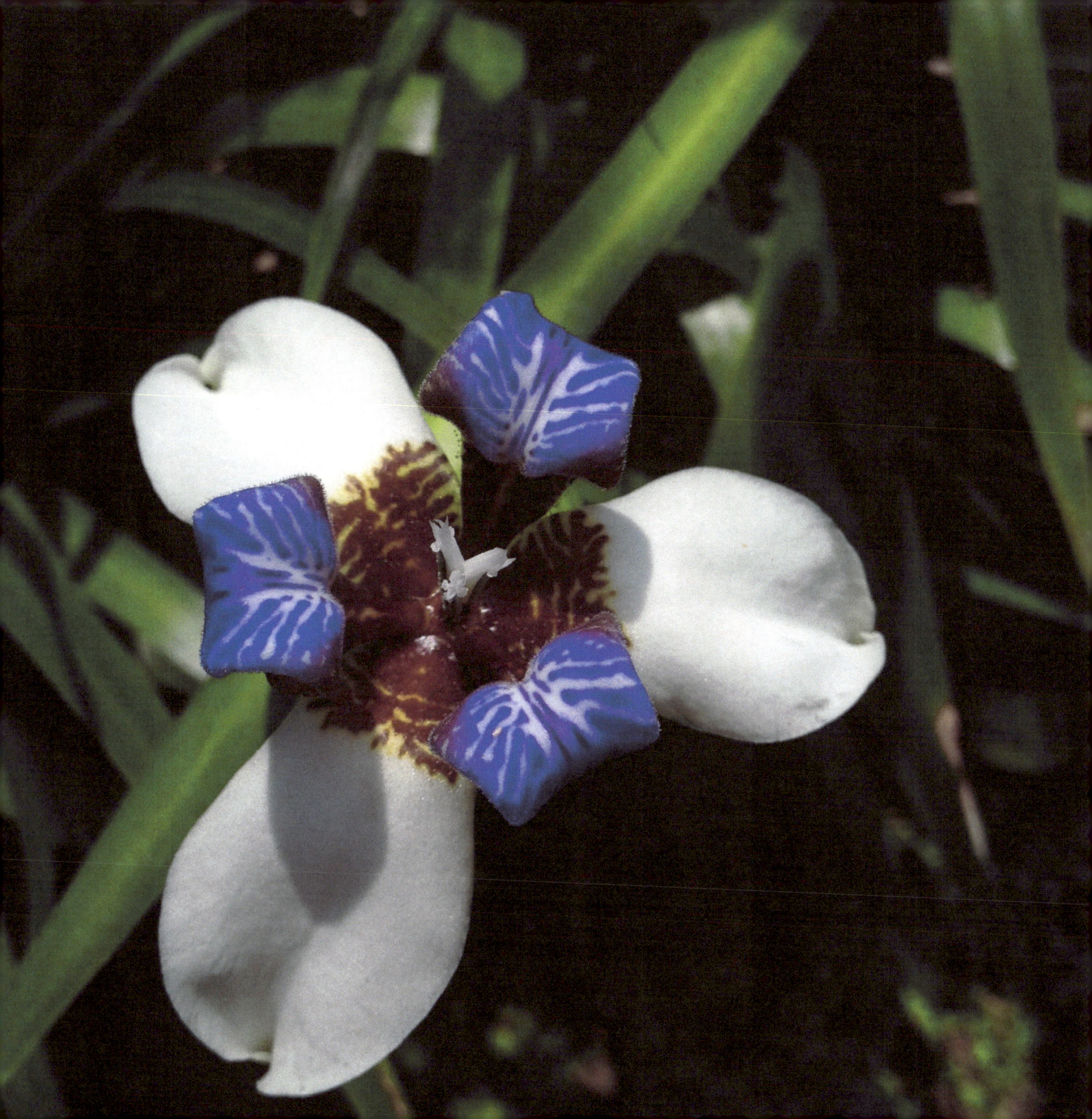

These are light blue flowers.

Estas son flores de color azul claro.

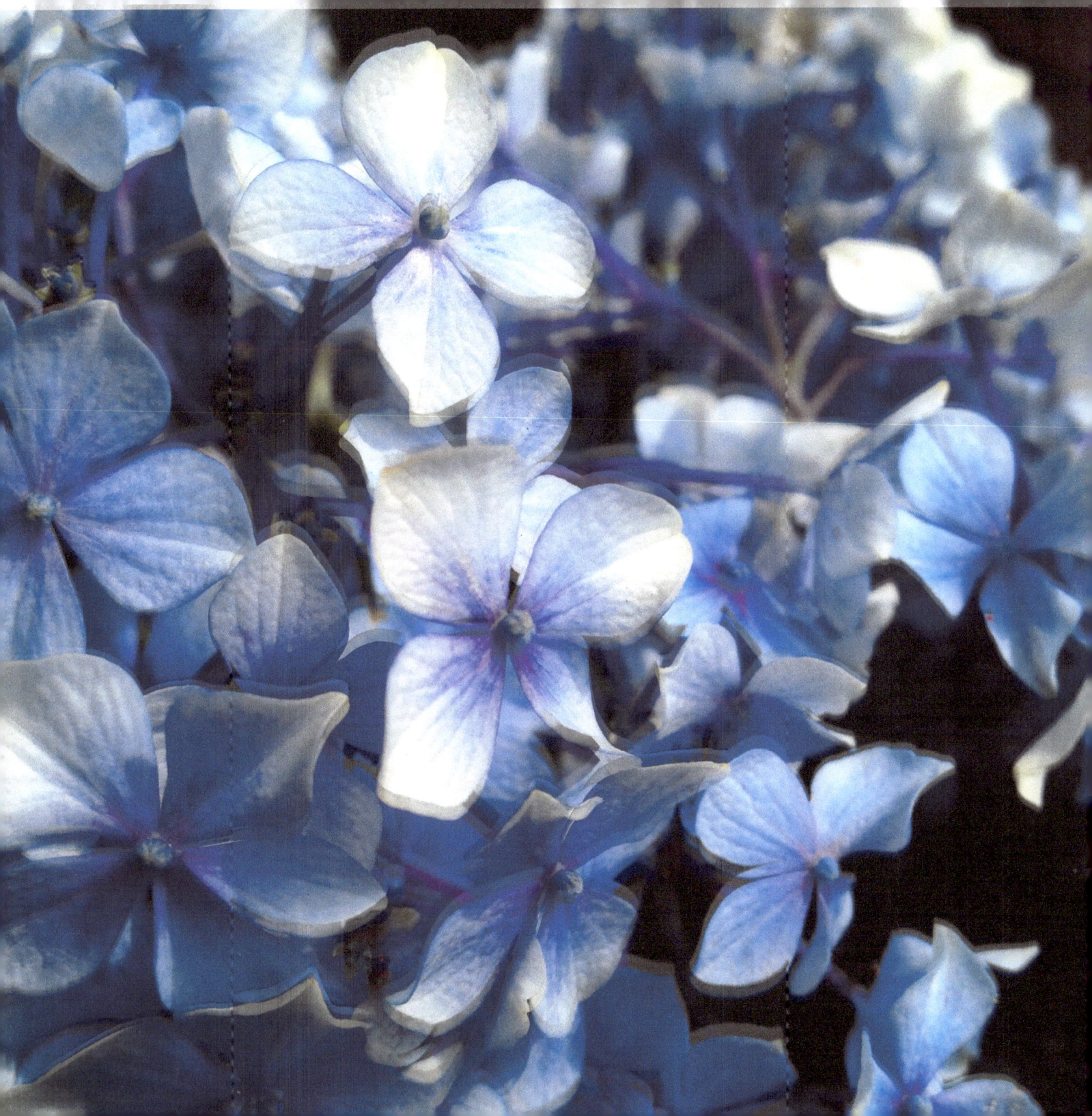

This is a
blue flower.


Esta es
una flor azul.

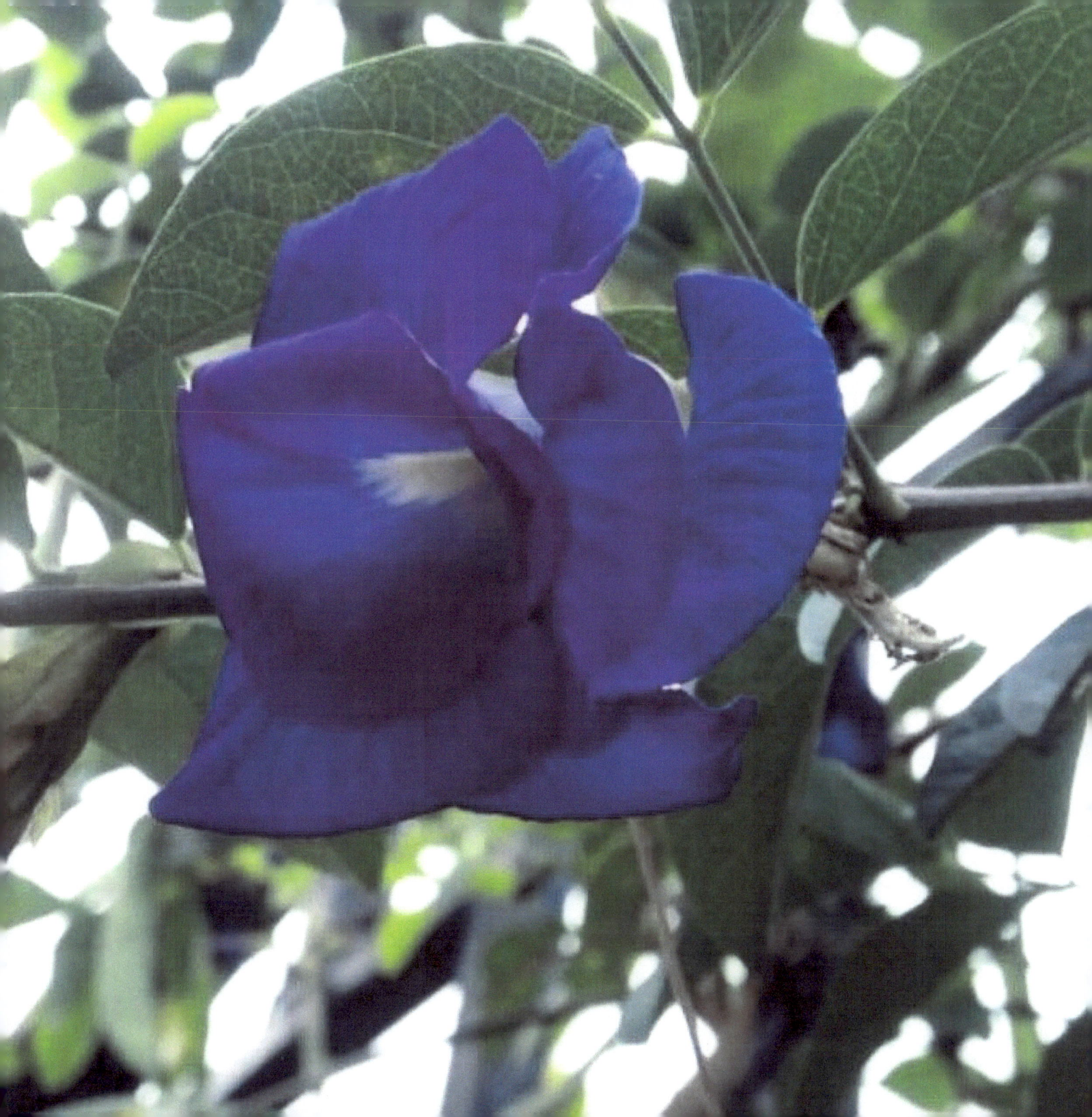

This is a dark purple flower.

Esta es una flor de color morado oscuro.

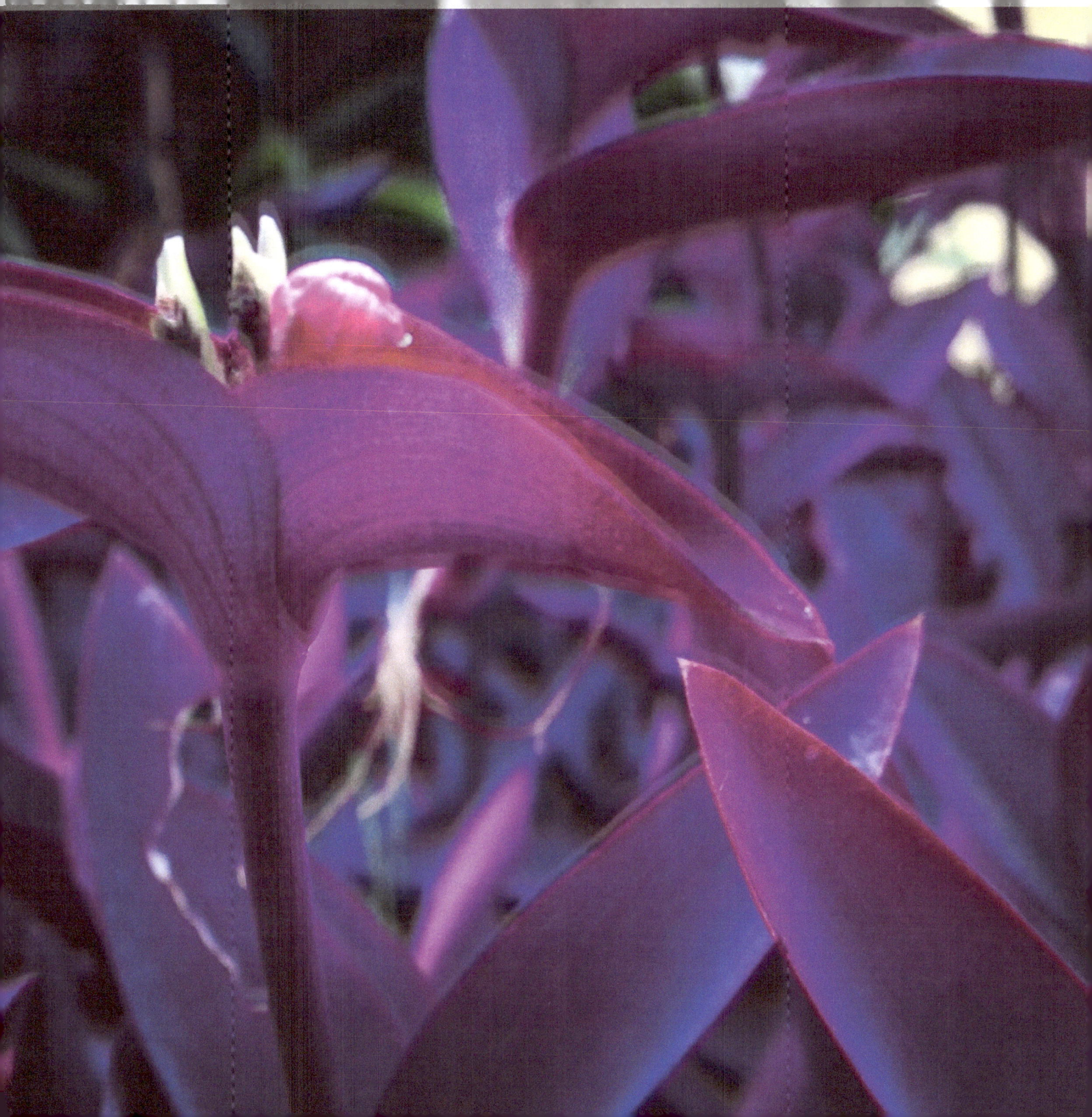

This is a bright purple flower.

Esta es una flor de color morado brillante.

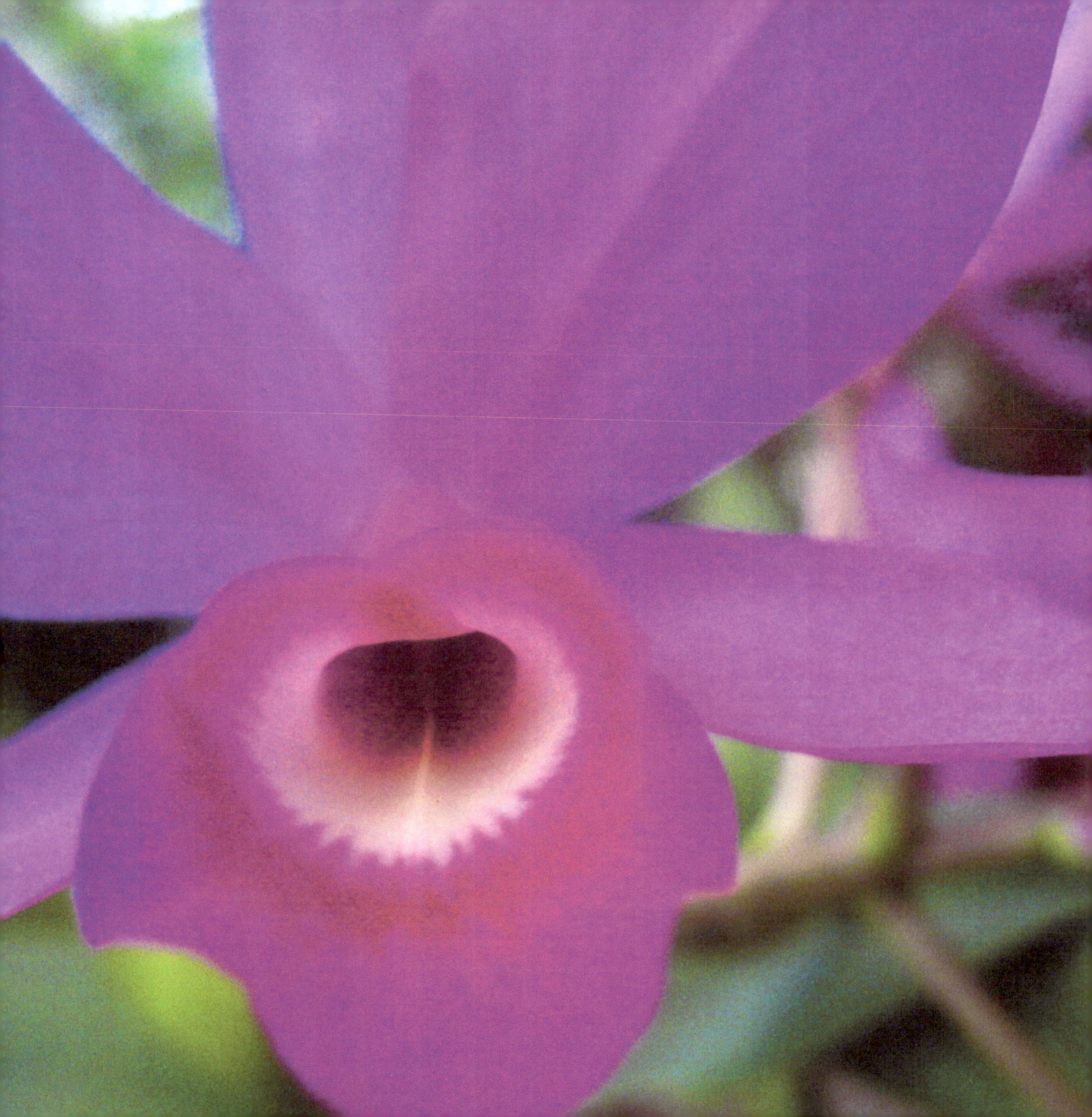

This is a light purple flower.

Esta es una flor de color morado claro.

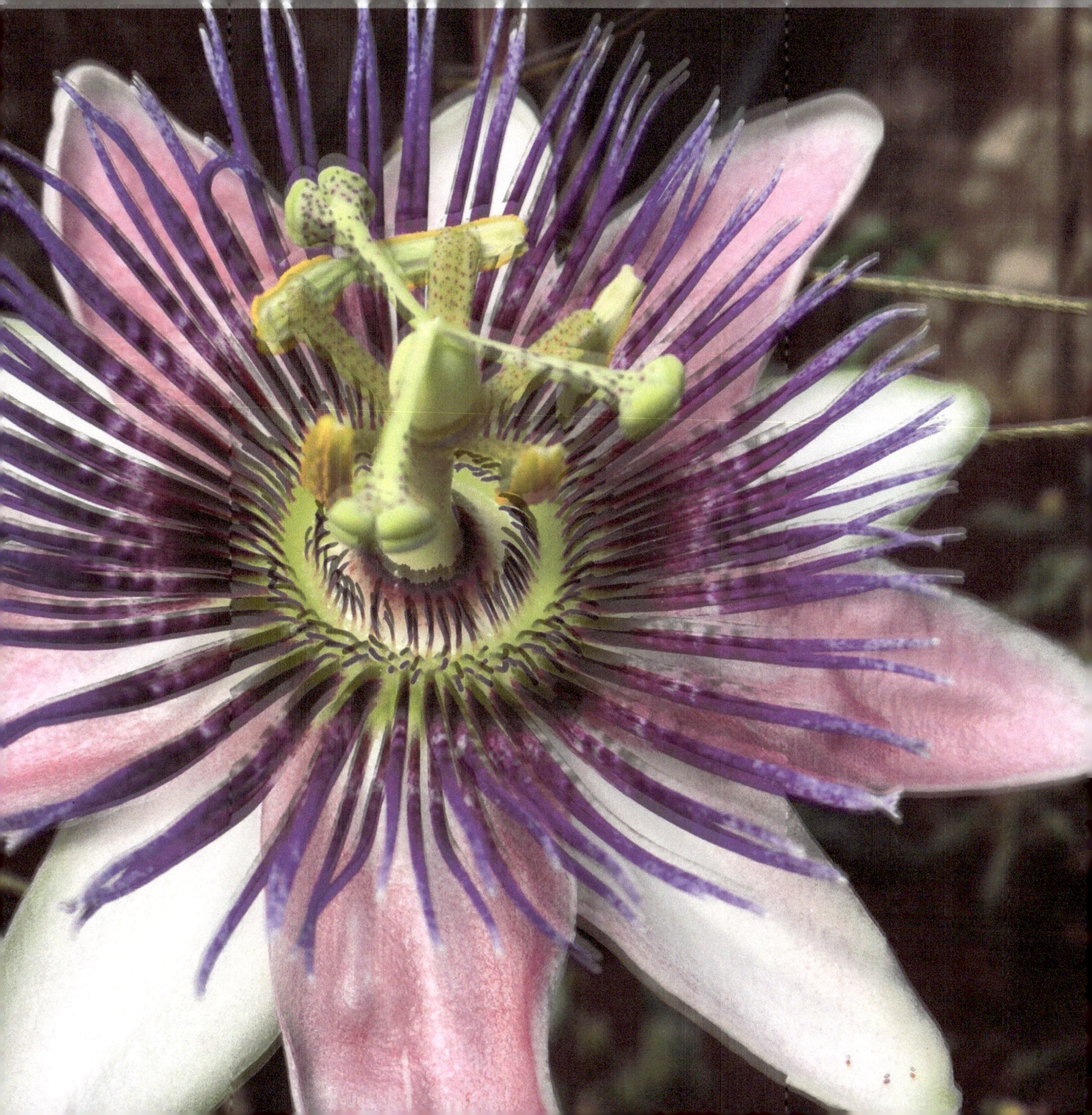

This is a pink flower.

Esta es una flor rosada.

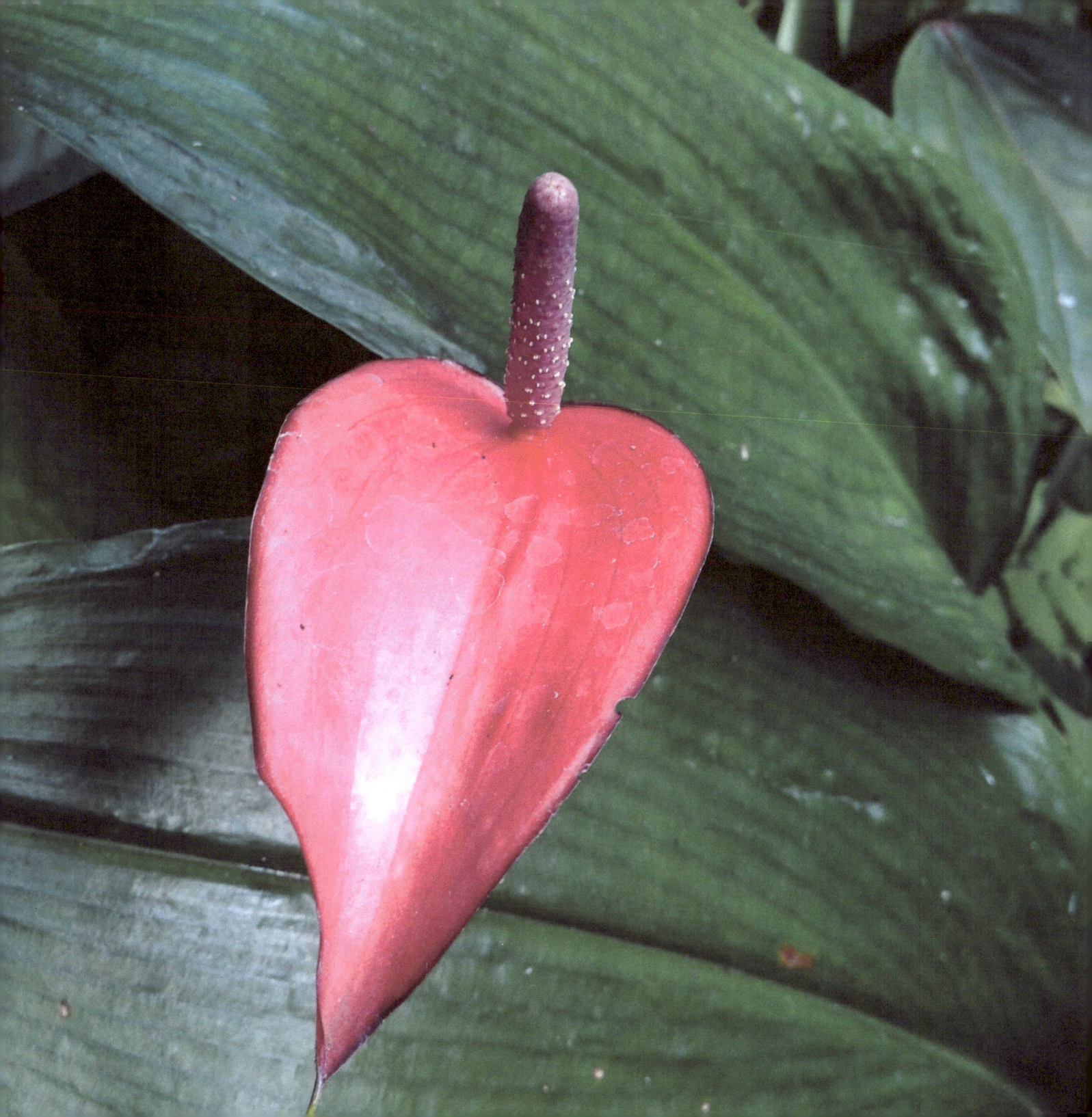

These are light pink flowers.

Estas son flores de color rosado claro.

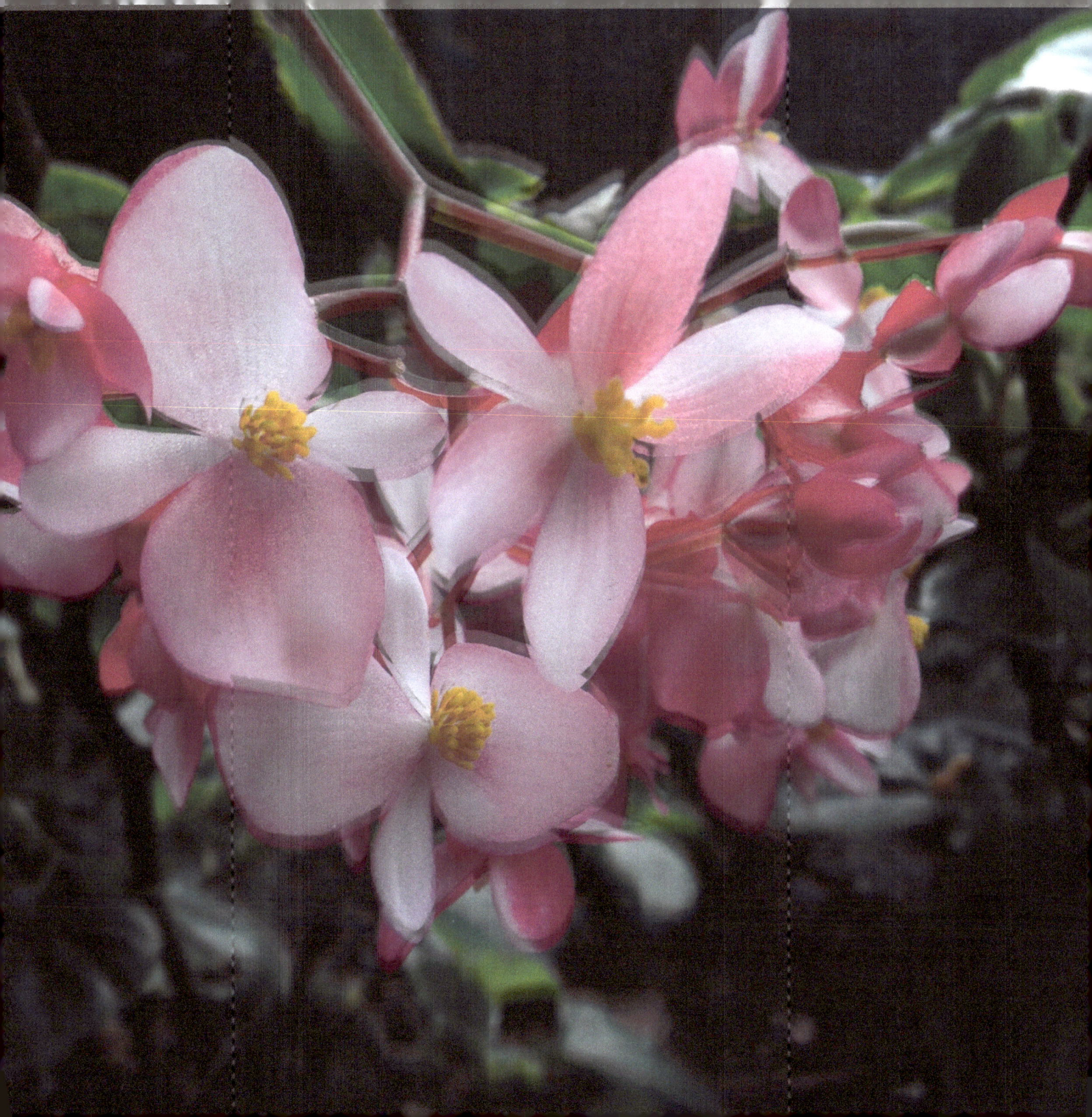

This is another pink flower.

Esta es otra flor rosada.

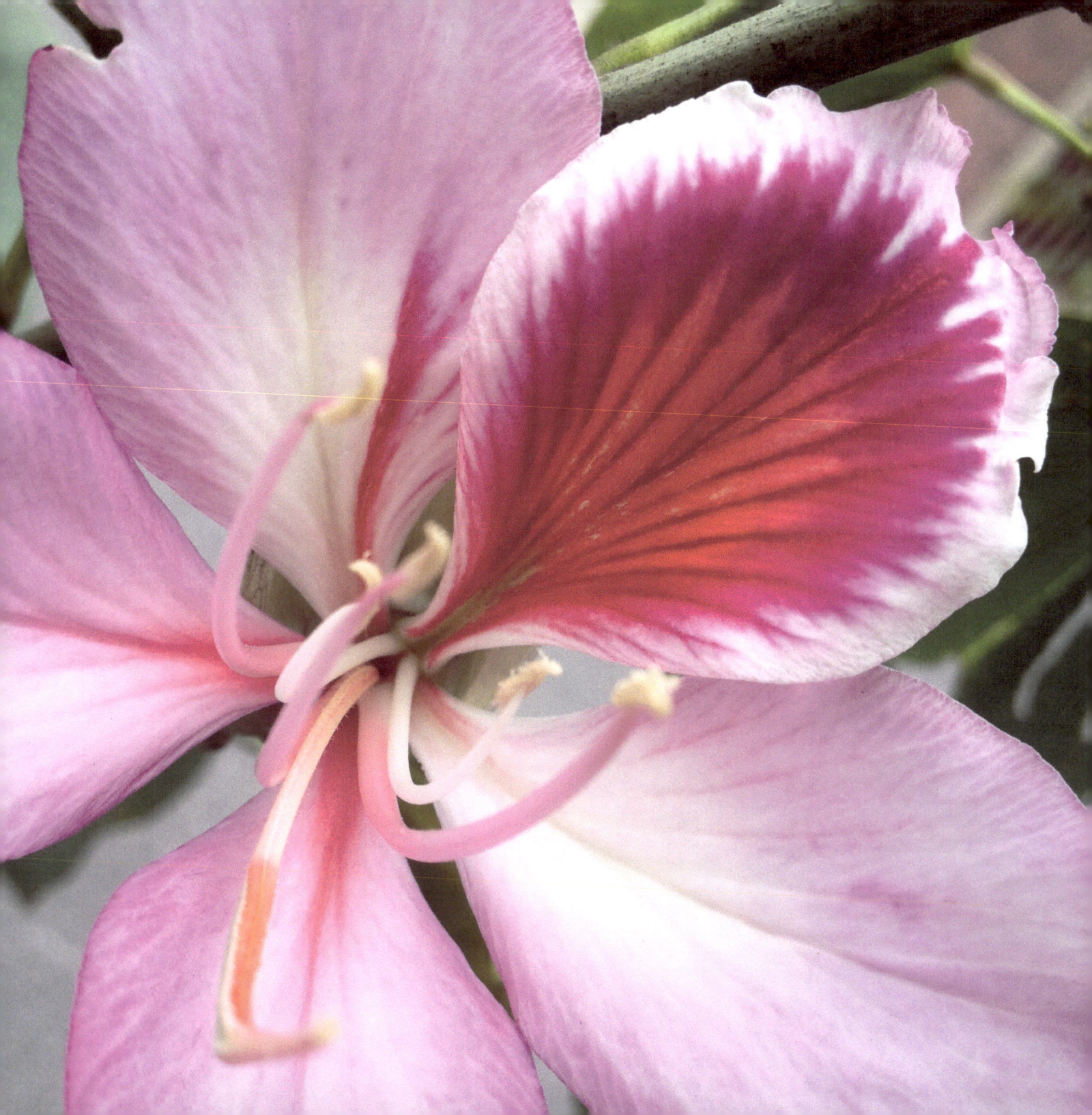

This is a
white flower.

Esta es una
flor blanca.

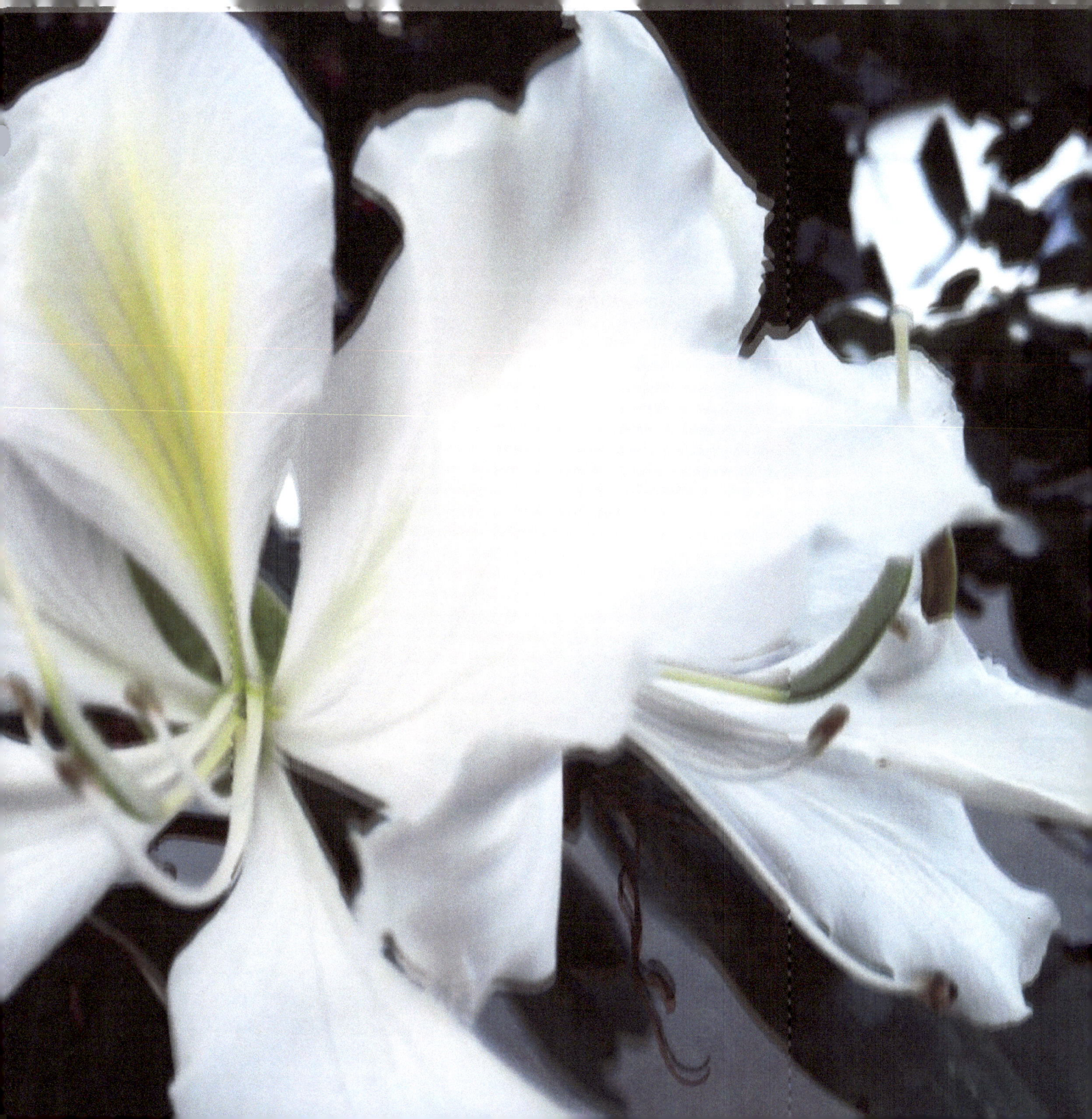

These are white flowers.

Estas son flores blancas.

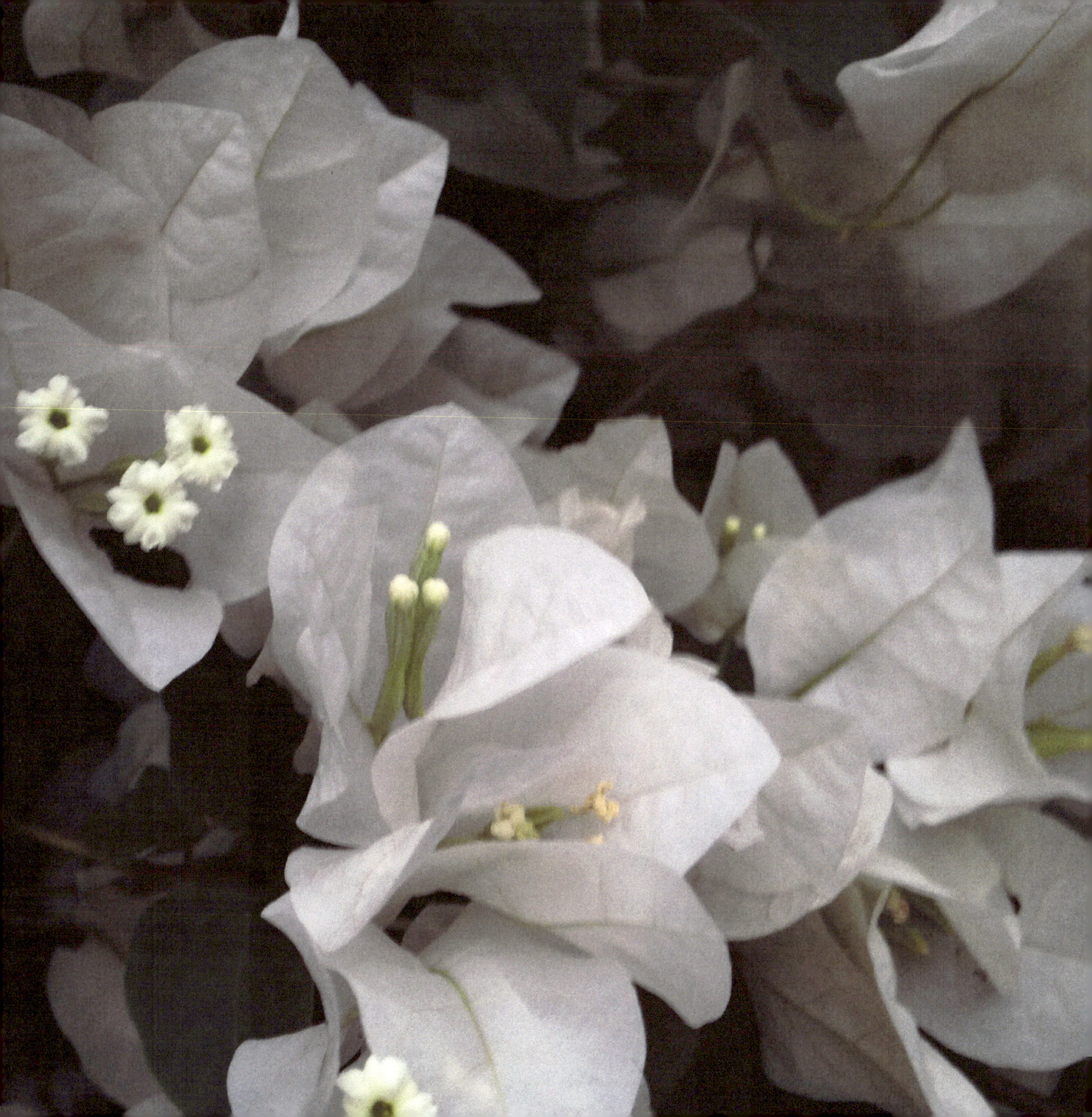

This is another white flower.

Esta es otra flor blanca.

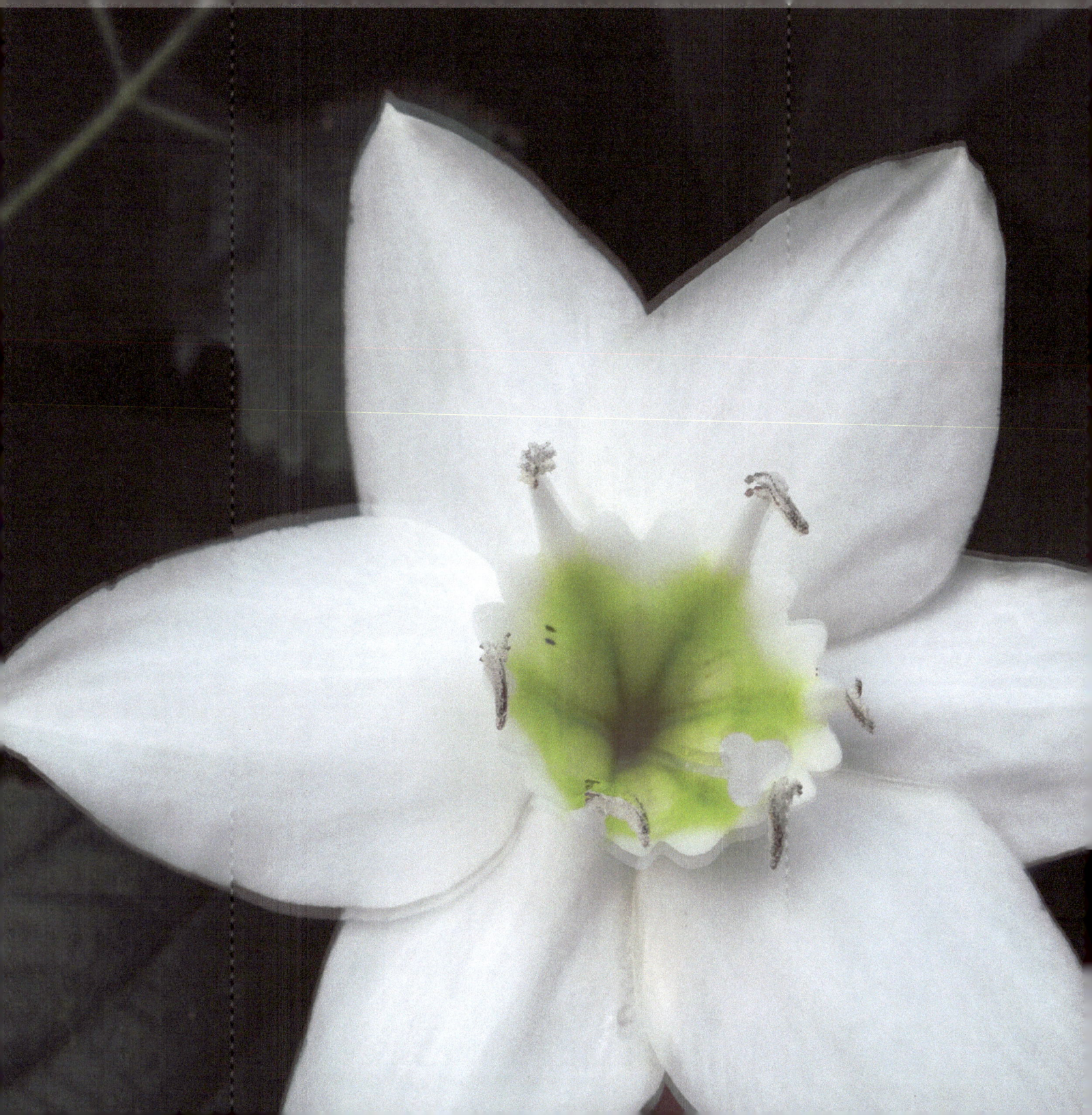

And what colors are these flowers?

¿Y qué colores tienen estas flores?

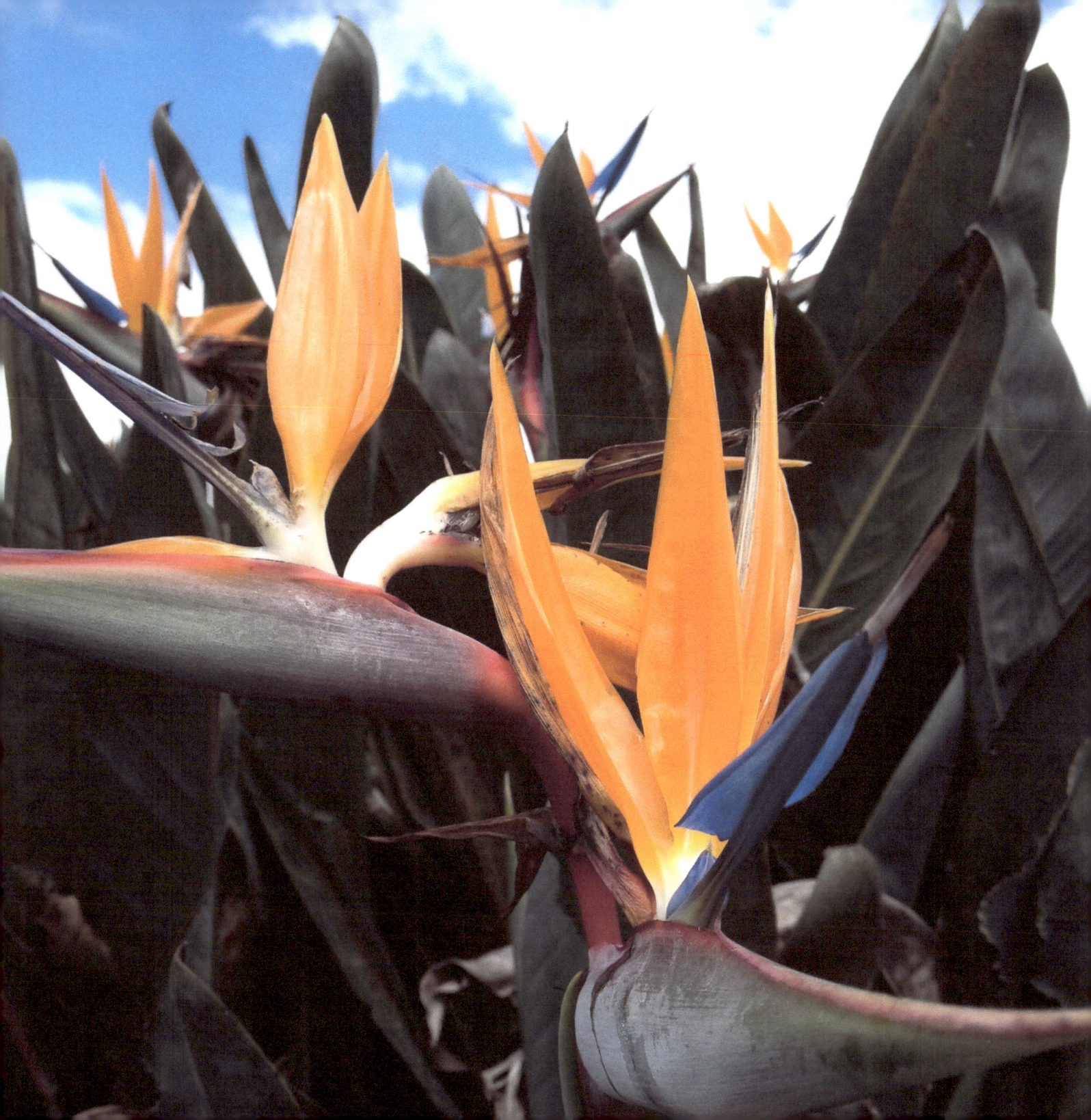

And this one?
What colors is it?

¿Y esta?
¿Qué colores tiene?

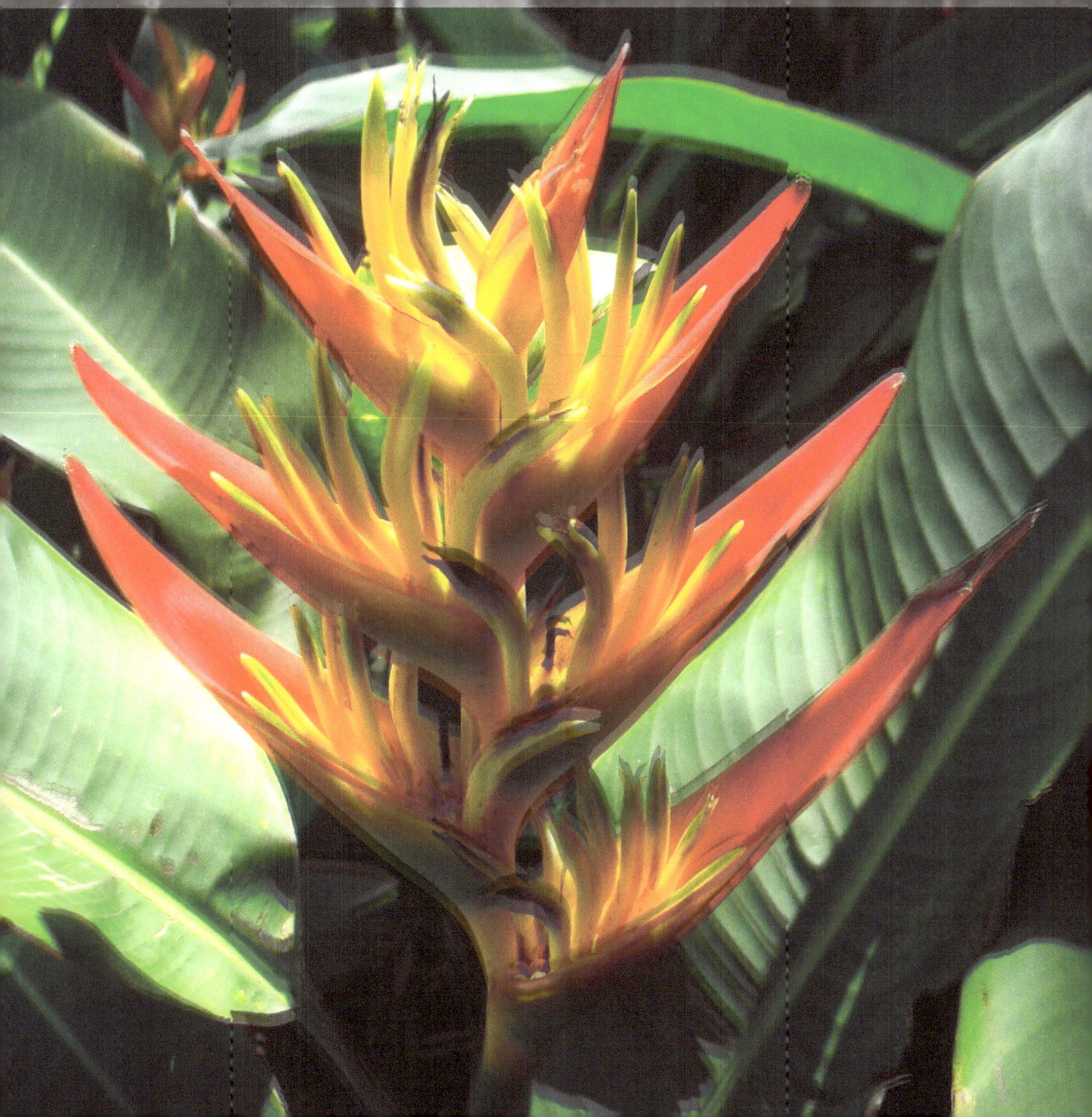

And these ones?
What colors are they?

¿Y estas?
¿Qué colores tienen?

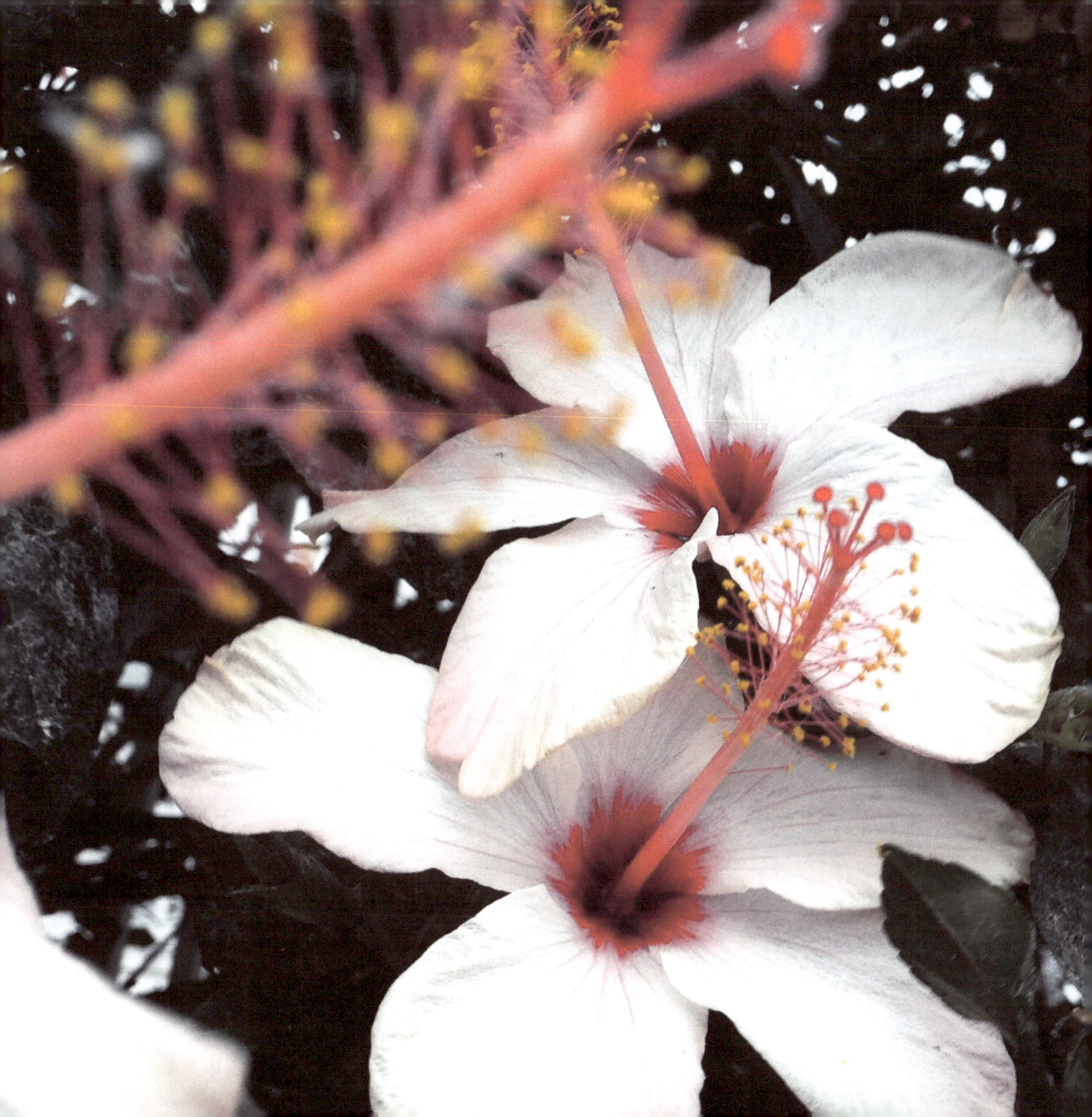

# BILINGUAL FLOWERS GUIDE BY COLOR & COMMON/SCIENTIFIC NAME

## RED/ROJO

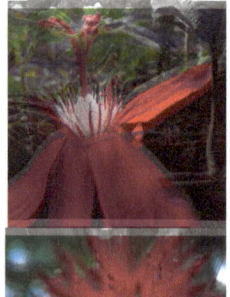

### Passion Flower
Pasión de Cristo
Passiflora

### Powder Puff
Plumerillo
Calliandra Haematocephala

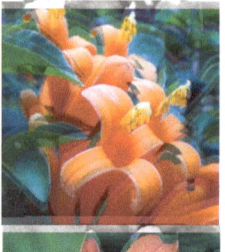

### Lobster's Claw
Heliconia Cascada
Heliconia Rostrata

## YELLOW/AMARILLO

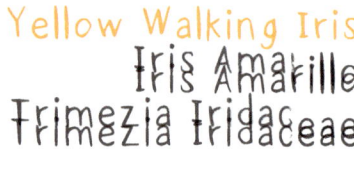

### Yellow Walking Iris
Iris Amarillo
Trimezia Iridaceae

### Canna Lily
Platanilla
Lillium

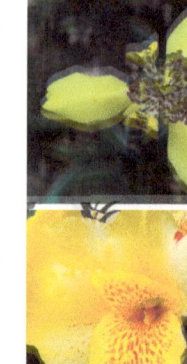

### Yellow Shrimp
Camarón Amarillo
Pachystachys Lutea

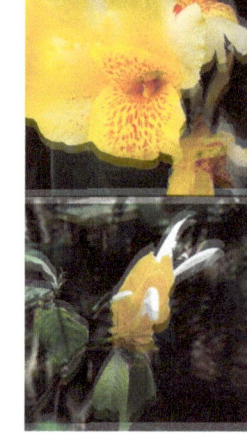

## ORANGE/ANARANJADO

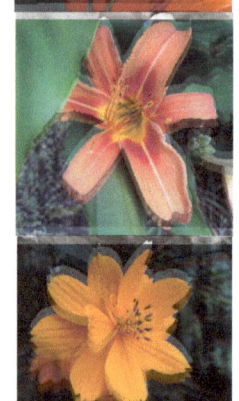

### Flaming Trumpet Vine
Triquitraque
Pyrostegia Venusta

### Orange Daylily
Lirio Naranja
Hemerocallis Aurantiaca

### Orange Cosmos
Cambray Anaranjado
Cosmos Sulphureus

## GREEN/VERDE

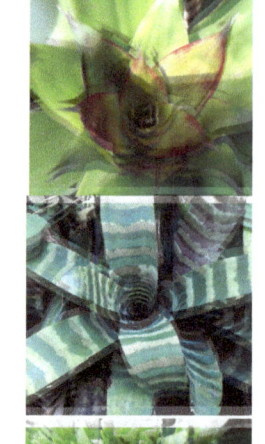

### Bromelia
Bromelia
Bromeliad

### Bromelia
Bromelia
Bromeliad

### Hydrangea
Hortensia
Hydrangea Macrophylla

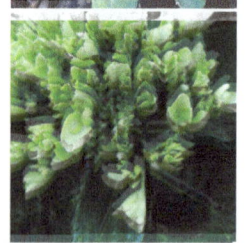

## BLUE/AZUL

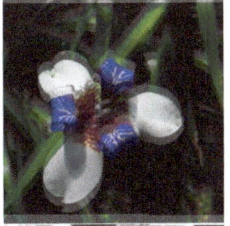
### Walking Iris
Iris Caminante
Neomarica Northiana

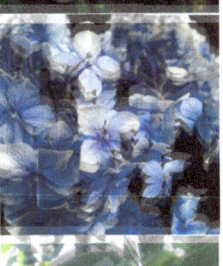
### Hydrangea
Hortensia
Hydrangea Macrophylla

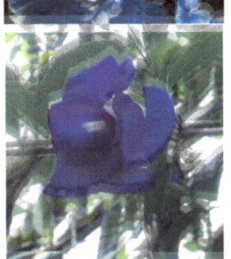
### Butterfly Pea
Conchita Azul
Clitoria Ternatea

## PINK/ROSADO

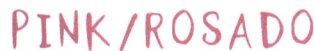

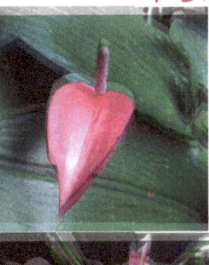
### Flamingo Lily
Anturio
Anthurium Andraeanum

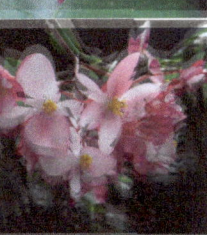
### Begonia
Begonia
Begonia Obliqua

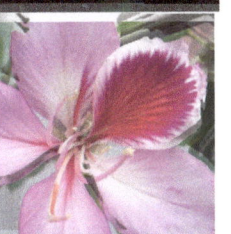
### Orchid Tree
Orquídea de Arbol
Bauhinia Purpurea

## PURPLE/MORADO

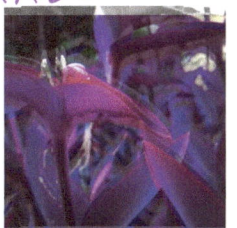
### Purple Heart
Purpurina
Tradescantia pallida

### Cattleya Orchid
Guaria Morada
Cattleya Skinneri

### Passion Flower
Passiflora
Passiflora Incarnata

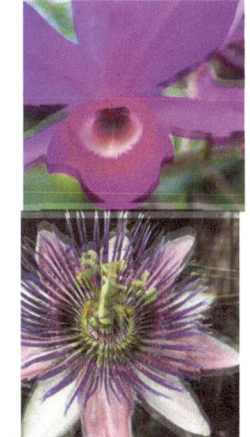

## WHITE/BLANCO

### White Ginger Lily
Lirio Blanco
Hedychium Coronarium

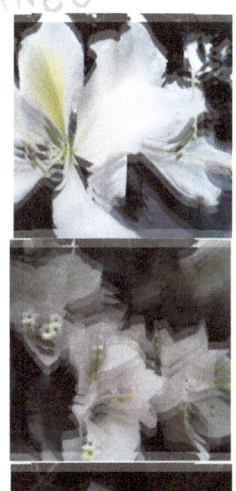

### Paper Flower
Veranera
Bougainvillea

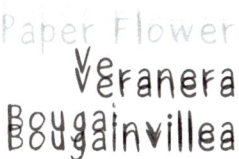

### Amazon Lily
Lirio del Amazonas
Eucharis Amazonica

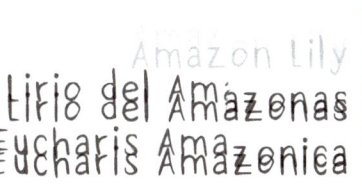

## MULTI-COLORED/MULTI-COLOR

## ANSWERS/RESPUESTAS

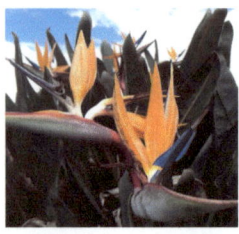

Birds of Paradise
Aves del Paraiso
Strelitzia Reginae

These flowers are orange, blue, red, green, and white

Estas flores tienen los colores de anaranjado, azul, rojo, verde, y blanco.

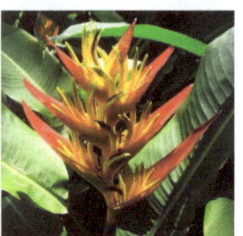

Parrot's Beak
Lorita
Heliconia Psittacorum

This flower is orange, red, yellow, and green

Esta flor tiene los colores de anaranjado, rojo, amarillo, y verde.

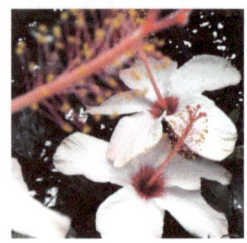

Hibiscus
Amapola
Hibiscus

These flowers are pink, white, and yellow.

Estas flores tienen los colores de rosado, blanco, y amarillo.

## SPANISH COLORS GRAMMAR LESSON

In English, there is only one way to say each color, but in Spanish there are four different ways to say each color. Red (rojo) will be used as an example.

1. Masculine singular - rojo
2. Feminine singular - roja
3. Masculine plural - rojos
4. Feminine plural - rojas

Also, adjectives and colors in Spanish always come after the noun, not before like in English. We say red flower, but they say flower red or flor roja.

| red flower | orange flowers | yellow flower | green flowers | blue flowers | pink flower | purple flowers | white flower |
|---|---|---|---|---|---|---|---|
| flor roja | flores anaranjadas | flor amarilla | flores verdes | flores azules | flor rosada | flores moradas | flor blanca |

www.ingramcontent.com/pod-product-compliance
Lightning Source LLC
Chambersburg PA
CBHW051920210526
45473CB00006B/2079